FamilyCircle

BIG BOOK OF CHRISTMAS

GREAT HOLIDAY RECIPES, GIFTS, AND DECORATING IDEAS

A LEISURE ARTS PUBLICATION

FamilyCircle BIG BOOK OF christmas

Library of Congress Catalog Number 98-66514
Hardcover ISBN 1-57486-190-5
Softcover ISBN 1-57486-191-3

10 9 8 7 6 5 4 3 2 1

THE MOST wonderful TIME OF THE YEAR

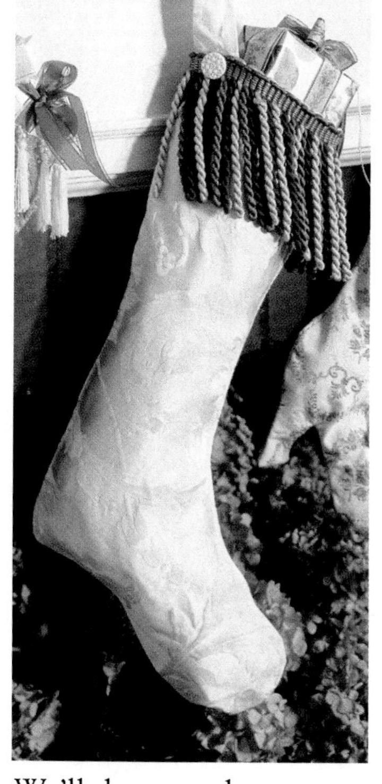

Working with our talented team of editors each year to put together all the elements of a spectacular holiday celebration is one of the most challenging — and delightful! — parts of my job. Our goal is simple: To create the merriest mix of crafts, decorations, and recipes possible, so you can turn our ideas into your best Christmas ever.

This beautiful volume will help you celebrate the first Christmas of an exciting new century. Why not choose an overall theme for your family's festivities? Whether your decorating taste is embellish-everything Victorian, a rustic Mother-Nature motif, or somewhere in-between, this book offers all the how-to's you need. And no matter what the theme, whether you're a beginning or advanced crafter, you'll find our treasury of keepsakes to your liking. We'll show you how to turn painted jingle bells into cheerful Snowman Necklaces for guests, stitch up spiffy his-and-hers hostess vests, and much more.

In the mood for scrumptious new recipes? Our *Big Book of Christmas* contains plenty to please your heart and palate — from a Bright & Early Brunch and elegant-but-easy dinners (both traditional and progressive-style) to irresistible cookies, cakes, and pies your clan will clamor for in Decembers to come. There are also over 20 terrific gifts from the kitchen, including Chocolate-Dipped Pretzels and Maple-Nut Rugelach.

I truly believe we've captured the wonder of the season in this special holiday book. I sincerely hope that our *Family Circle Big Book of Christmas* will inspire the spirit of joy and giving in you and yours.

Susan Ungaro

Susan Ungaro
Editor-in-Chief, Family Circle

contents

a christmas welcome

DRESS THE DOOR — FRONT OR BACK — IN FESTIVE STYLE TO WELCOME ONE AND ALL. LOOK BEYOND THE USUAL EVERGREENS... TRY FLOWERS AND FRUITS FOR AN EYE-CATCHING ARRANGEMENT. THE SMALLEST EFFORT CAN HAVE A MAGICAL EFFECT!

Greet your guests with this plush North Star, perfect for wishing upon.

How-To's on page 118

Plaided pinecones with ho-ho bows and a ribboned wreath would be inviting additions to a door plaque (above). *Elegant spiral trees* (opposite) *festooned in Della Robbia-style with faux fruit and gleaming ribbons stand sentry by the front door. A mistletoe-trimmed garland and fruited swags complete the ensemble.*

RUSTIC WELCOME PLAQUE

You need: straight twigs for plaque – about 1/2" and 1/4" dia.; twigs for "Welcome"; birch bark; glue gun; hammer; finishing nails; pruning shears; evergreen cones; red ribbon; plaid ribbon; string; 12" evergreen wreath.

Cutting twigs for plaque: Cut the following lengths of 1/2" dia. twigs – five 24"L, five 12 1/2"L, two 4 1/2"L, and four 6 1/2"L. Cut the following 1/4" dia. twigs: three 2"L, two 5"L. When assembling plaque, trim twigs to fit as needed using pruning shears.

Assembling plaque base: Follow Plaque Base Diagram (page 119) to arrange 12 1/2"L twigs on a flat surface. Glue 16 1/2"L twigs along ends of 12 1/2"L twigs. Glue two 24"L long twigs on top of 12 1/2"L twigs. Glue 4 1/2"L, then 6 1/2"L twigs to sides of plaque to complete shape. Use finishing nails as needed to hold plaque base firmly together. Nail finishing nails to 12 1/2"L twigs as shown.

Assembling plaque shelf: Space 2"L twigs 6" apart on flat surface. Glue remaining 24"L twigs as shown in Shelf Diagram A (page 119). Glue shelf to plaque base using 5"L twigs for support as shown in Shelf Diagram B (page 119).

Making "Welcome" sign: Cut a 3"x18" piece of birch bark. Cut small twigs to fit along short edges and one long edge; glue. Cut small twigs to spell out "Welcome." Glue to bark. Glue sign to front edge of plaque shelf.

Decorating cones: Glue center of a 14" length of plaid ribbon to base of each cone; knot ribbon ends together. Glue a bow tied from red decorative ribbon to each cone.

How-To's continued on page 118

GILDED FINIAL WREATH

You need: assorted decorative wooden pieces (spindles, medallions, etc.); spray sealer; acrylic paint – white, metallic gold; paintbrushes; disposable rags; artificial evergreen wreath; 1½"W decorative ribbon; 1"W gold mesh ribbon; gold ball ornaments; gold faceted star ornaments; glue gun; floral wire.

Decorating wooden pieces: Spray pieces with sealer. Dilute white paint with water to an ink-like consistency. Paint wooden pieces with diluted paint. Before paint dries, wipe off excess with a rag, leaving paint in crevices for a white-washed effect. Dry-brush wooden pieces with gold paint. If desired, dry-brush wooden pieces with additional undiluted white paint.

Decorating wreath: Wrap 1½"W ribbon around wreath; glue in place. Tie gold mesh ribbon into small bows. Glue bows to bottoms of spindles. Glue wooden pieces and stars to wreath. Wire ball ornaments to wreath.

How-To's continued on page 119

Almost anything can be drawn into a charming wreath! (Opposite) *A trip to a home center will yield wooden spindles, medallions, faceted stars, and other accents that you can gild, then add to gathered greenery. Give dried hydrangeas a light coating of gold or silver spray for this fabulous floral wreath* (top), *or twine sprays of eucalyptus, boxwood, euonymus, and cocculus leaves into a stunning single-color display* (bottom).

retro regalia

CELEBRATE THE FIFTIES WITH RETRO REGALIA AND BLAST-FROM-THE-PAST FARE! EVEN IF YOU MISSED THE MID-CENTURY THE FIRST TIME AROUND, YOU CAN EASILY RE-CREATE THIS PLAYFUL CHRISTMAS PAST.

Enjoy the classic combination of red and white. Don't forget to put a treat in each pocket of this Advent calendar, sewn from vintage-print fabric (opposite). Jolly snow dolls, made from plush felt, are ready for the slopes! Give her a stylish bonnet, him a dapper topper.

How-To's on page 120

Bold, bright poinsettias, popular back then, are just as festive now. Trim the tree skirt with motifs cut from a fifties-era tablecloth. (Opposite) On the tree, mingle trims old and new. Use reproduction prints for the fabric globes and prancing pony ornaments. Twine chenille-ball fringe around the branches, then cap it all off with a jingle-belled Santa hat.

CANDY CANE ORNAMENTS

You need: Wooden candy-cane shapes; sandpaper; paintbrushes; gesso; acrylic paints – white, red; craft glue; crystal glitter.

Painting: Coat canes with gesso. Let dry; sand. Paint white; let dry. Paint 1/2" red stripes diagonally on canes. Dip brush handle in white paint to paint dots on red stripes; let dry.

Finishing: Thin glue slightly with water. Apply glue to top edge of each cane. Sprinkle glitter into glue; let dry. Shake off excess.

POINSETTIA TREE SKIRT

You need: Vintage-print square tablecloth; drawing compass.

To do: Fold tablecloth in half from top to bottom and again from left to right. Set compass to 2". Insert point of compass in top left corner of tablecloth and mark an arc. Cut out through all layers to form center opening. Unfold. For back opening, cut a straight line from center of one edge to center opening. Hem all raw edges.

How-To's continued on page 122

HO HO HO

Set out nostalgic block ornaments (right), *decoupaged with vintage greeting card cutouts or stickers. A bead nose, pearl buttons, and wool scarf dress up our oh-so-cool snowman. Raid the attic for fabric to create hankie pillows* (below). *Doilies, pom-poms, and fringe fancy up all sizes of cuffed stockings* (opposite), *while painted beads stack into merry candlesticks for the mantel. Add some wooden candy cane ornaments to a wreath.*

BLOCK ORNAMENTS

You need: 2" wooden blocks; sandpaper; paintbrushes; gesso; acrylic paints in assorted colors; small scissors; vintage-style Christmas cards; decoupage medium; crystal glitter; perle cotton; buttons.

Preparing blocks: Sand blocks to round edges and corners. Coat with gesso; let dry. Sand.

Painting: Paint blocks in desired colors; let dry.

Decoupaging: Cut motifs from cards. Coat back of each motif with decoupage medium; press onto blocks. Paint dots around motifs, if desired; let dry. Coat blocks with decoupage medium; sprinkle with glitter. Let dry.

Finishing: Cut 10" of perle cotton per block. Thread ends through button holes; knot into hanging loop. Glue button to top of block to make ornament.

How-To's continued on page 123

BOW-TRIMMED BOOTIE

You need: 1/2 yd checked-print fabric; 1/4 yd red-print fabric; 2 yds of 1"W gingham ribbon.

Cutting: Enlarge pattern (page 125). From checked fabric, cut two stocking sections for front and back. From print fabric, cut one 16" x 5" cuff.

Sewing: (***Note:*** All stitching is done in 1/4" seams, with right sides facing and raw edges even, unless noted.) Pin and stitch front to back along sides and lower edges, leaving upper edge open. Clip curves; turn. Fold cuff in half crosswise; stitch short ends together. Slip cuff over upper edge of stocking. Pin and stitch one edge of cuff to upper edge of stocking, aligning seams. Turn under 1/4" on other cuff edge; fold to inside of stocking, over cuff seam. Hand-stitch fold over seam. Fold cuff to right side of stocking.

How-To's continued on page 123

String pony beads onto pipe cleaners; twist into a tiny beaded tree and "plant" in a foam ball inside a painted pot (right)*; heap cinnamon candies on top. Mix jolly prints to whip up a cozy quilt* (opposite) *or cover a photo album* (below)*. Clip stitchery from vintage table linens, or choose your favorite embroidery pattern to adorn the album.*

BEAD TREE FAVOR

You need: Small clay pot; white spray paint; red paint marker; plastic foam ball to fit in pot; green and white chenille stems; wire cutters; assorted Christmas-colored pony beads; cinnamon candies.

Preparing pot: Paint pot white. Add red dots with paint marker. Wedge plastic foam ball into pot.

Making tree: Cut a green chenille stem about twice as tall as pot for tree trunk. String beads onto trunk, leaving bottom of trunk undecorated. String beads onto four lengths of white chenille stems, then wrap center of each stem around trunk to form branches. Trim branches to desired length.

Finishing: Insert trunk into plastic foam. Cover foam with candies.

How-To's continued on page 130

Christmas
Santa's Helper

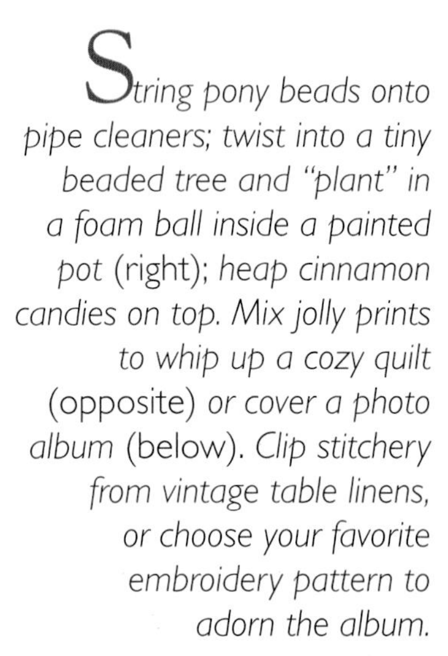

String pony beads onto pipe cleaners; twist into a tiny beaded tree and "plant" in a foam ball inside a painted pot (right); *heap cinnamon candies on top. Mix jolly prints to whip up a cozy quilt* (opposite) *or cover a photo album* (below). *Clip stitchery from vintage table linens, or choose your favorite embroidery pattern to adorn the album.*

BEAD TREE FAVOR

You need: Small clay pot; white spray paint; red paint marker; plastic foam ball to fit in pot; green and white chenille stems; wire cutters; assorted Christmas-colored pony beads; cinnamon candies.

Preparing pot: Paint pot white. Add red dots with paint marker. Wedge plastic foam ball into pot.

Making tree: Cut a green chenille stem about twice as tall as pot for tree trunk. String beads onto trunk, leaving bottom of trunk undecorated. String beads onto four lengths of white chenille stems, then wrap center of each stem around trunk to form branches. Trim branches to desired length.

Finishing: Insert trunk into plastic foam. Cover foam with candies.

How-To's continued on page 130

BOW-TRIMMED BOOTIE

You need: 1/2 yd checked-print fabric; 1/4 yd red-print fabric; 2 yds of 1"W gingham ribbon.

Cutting: Enlarge pattern (page 125). From checked fabric, cut two stocking sections for front and back. From print fabric, cut one 16" x 5" cuff.

Sewing: (***Note:*** All stitching is done in 1/4" seams, with right sides facing and raw edges even, unless noted.) Pin and stitch front to back along sides and lower edges, leaving upper edge open. Clip curves; turn. Fold cuff in half crosswise; stitch short ends together. Slip cuff over upper edge of stocking. Pin and stitch one edge of cuff to upper edge of stocking, aligning seams. Turn under 1/4" on other cuff edge; fold to inside of stocking, over cuff seam. Hand-stitch fold over seam. Fold cuff to right side of stocking.

How-To's continued on page 123

NAPKIN PILLOWS

You need (for each): 2 fabric napkins (same size); fiberfill stuffing.
To do: Place napkins wrong sides together. Stitch together 1" from edges, leaving an opening for stuffing. Stuff with fiberfill. Sew opening closed.

HOLIDAY NAPKINS

You need: White cotton napkins; holiday cookie cutters; air-fading fabric marker; embroidery floss – red, green.
Embroidering: Place cookie cutter in corner of napkin; trace outline with marker. Using six strands of floss sew running stitches along marked lines. Working over the same number of threads each time, make a row of cross-stitches along inner edge of hem on each side of napkin, making stitches about 1/4" high.

How-To's continued on page 128

Great for giving…or keeping! Napkin pillows (above) *couldn't be quicker — take two hemmed squares, stitch up three sides, stuff, and sew closed. Cookie cutters provide the patterns for a set of stitched napkins* (right). *Pack in a basket, along with cutlery.* (Opposite) *To keep a holiday chef and assistant neat in the kitchen, appliqué fun Santa and elf aprons.*

victorian beauties

IF YOU THINK YOU CAN NEVER HAVE TOO MANY DECORATIONS, STEP BACK TO THE VICTORIAN ERA, WHEN OVER-THE-TOP WAS THE ORDER OF THE DAY. THE TREE WAS LADEN WITH ELABORATE TRIMS; THE ENTIRE HOUSE WAS ADORNED WITH SUMPTUOUS LITTLE TOUCHES. THE MOOD WAS FORMAL, FESTIVE, AND OH-SO-GRAND!

A fashionable mantel might have borne stockings such as these: (from left) a trinket-trimmed brocade boot, a velvet-cuffed high-button shoe, a multicolored fringed bootie, and a tasseled silk and pearl stocking.

How-To's on page 131

Wrap up lots of ribbon balls to tumble in a vintage hatbox, as well as dangle from the tree. (Opposite) Think opulence for the tree: Stream glittery ribbon from bough to bough, place puffs of hydrangea amidst ornaments both store-bought and handmade. Seat a glorious golden angel atop to oversee all.

RIBBON BALLS

You need: 3" plastic foam balls; assorted ribbons; pins.
Assembling: Wrap ribbon around ball; pin at top. Trim ribbon close to pin. Attach remaining ribbons in same way to cover ball.
Finishing: Cut 7" of ribbon for hanging loop; pin ends to ball. Cut 12" of ribbon; tie in bow. Pin at base of hanging loop.

CROCHETED BONNETS

You need: 6" crocheted doll bonnets; antique gold spray paint; narrow ribbon; glue gun; dried rosebuds; dried hydrangea blossoms.
Assembling: Spray-paint bonnets; let dry. Cut 8" of ribbon for each bonnet. Glue ribbon around each bonnet for band. Glue rosebuds and hydrangea to each bonnet.

CROCHETED ANGELS

You need: 8" crocheted angels; metallic gold spray paint; paintbrush; decoupage medium; gold glitter.
Assembling: Spray-paint angels; let dry. Brush decoupage medium along edges of wings and bottoms of skirts; sprinkle generously with glitter. Let dry; shake off excess.

BROCADE DOVES

You need (for each): Brocade upholstery fabric; chalk pencil; fiberfill stuffing.
Cutting: Enlarge patterns (page 135). Cut two body sections, two tail sections and one gusset from fabric. Transfer markings.

How-To's continued on page 134

Embellish the tree (opposite) *with crocheted bonnets and angels, craft-store finds that you spray gold, then deck with dried blossoms, faux pearls, and rose ribbon. You can fashion a flock of brocade doves to alight among the branches. Loop brocade and satin into a treeful of resplendent ribbon rosettes.* (Below) *Gold and botanical-print wraps are in keeping with the period. To display these rich gifts, sew our Victorian tree skirt from champagne jacquard, stitched together with ribbon and bustled with bows.*

How-To's on page 134

CHRISTMAS THROW

You need: 60"W fabric – 1½ yds gold velvet, 1½ yds tapestry; twin-size quilt batting; silk ribbon – 5½ yds plus 10" per flower of ¾"W green with rust edge, 15" per flower of 1"W sheer bronze, 4" per leaf of ½"W sheer moss.

Cutting: Cut one 52" x 54" piece of velvet and one 52" x 54" piece of tapestry fabric for front and back.

Assembling: Place velvet (front of throw) right side up. Starting at one corner, pin on green/rust ribbon, placing outer edge of ribbon 1" from edges of velvet. Fold ribbon at 90-degree angle at each corner, forming miters. Turn under end of ribbon; stitch ribbon to velvet along both long edges. Center tapestry (back of throw), face up, on batting; baste edges. Trim batting even with tapestry. Place velvet, face down, over tapestry, raw edges even. Stitch edges in ½" seams, leaving opening along one side. Trim away batting within seam allowance; trim corners of all fabric. Turn; slipstitch opening closed.

Making flowers and leaves: For each green/rust flower, cut 10" of ribbon. For each bronze flower, cut 15" of ribbon. For each leaf, cut 4" of moss-colored ribbon. Hand-sew running stitches along one long edge of each flower ribbon; pull up thread to gather ribbon into circle, forming flower. Make several small stitches to secure ribbon ends; trim excess thread. Cross ends of each leaf ribbon to form loop; make several small stitches at base. Trim excess thread.

Finishing: Arrange flowers and leaves as desired on velvet; hand-stitch in place.

How-To's continued on page 134

Fit for a queen, the sumptuous Victorian Christmas throw (opposite) *teams amber velvet with a timeless tapestry fabric; ribbon buds bloom at each corner for a very royal touch.* (Left) *Tuck berries and roses in a slender vase, then wrap with paper wound round with gold cord and floral braid; hang from a doorknob. A plush velvet pillow* (below) *provides the family pet with a throne all his own. Then make a matching treat sack and fill it with the lucky dog's favorite goodies!*

naturally christmas

CREATE A GLORIOUS SETTING WITH NATURAL TRIMS...BOUGHS OF EVERGREEN, PINECONES, WHOLE SPICES, FRUITS BOTH REAL AND FAUX. FAMILY AND FRIENDS WILL CATCH THE CHRISTMAS SPIRIT THE MINUTE THEY WALK IN THE DOOR!

Festoon *the mantel* (opposite) *with a merry pinecone garland, shimmering with gold ball ornaments, and an eye-catching pinecone globe.* (Below) *Wrap your banister with greenery secured with thin wire; loosely twine with different-hued ribbons. Cut ribbon streamers and hot-glue pinecones to both ends; drape or knot around the garland and top with separate bows.*

How-To's on page 135

Topiaries of thyme, moss, or ivy (opposite) *make stunning tabletop displays. Buy or make the topiaries, wrap the pots in velvet, and ornament with ribbons and stars.* (Left) *Give kitchen chairs Christmas character — tie on tasseled cording caught up with the smallest papier-mâché fruit.* (Below) *Gild terra-cotta pots for candle holders that shine among patches of greenery; fill in between with a swirl of golden ribbon.*

How-To's on page 135

For a spectacular centerpiece, join clusters of roses, limes, pomegranates, and lemon leaves in a large terra-cotta planter or several smaller pots. (Opposite) An awning of Christmas plaid, punctuated with tassels, crowns an open cupboard. Line each shelf with wispy greenery.

FRUIT-AND-FLOWER POTS

You need: Sheet moss; terra-cotta pot; glue gun; craft knife; wood floral picks; dried lime wedges and slices; lemon leaves; 1 fresh lemon; pomegranates; pinecones; dried roses; florist's oasis.

Preparing pot: Place sheet moss, moss side down, on work surface. Apply glue to side of pot; roll pot in moss. Glue end of moss to pot; trim moss even with upper and lower edges of pot. Glue moss to cover empty spots.

Preparing embellishments: Arrange lime wedges, lime slices and lemon leaves in clusters; glue floral picks to clusters. Poke floral picks into bases of lemon and pomegranates. Glue pinecones, dried roses and additional leaves to floral picks in clusters.

Assembling: Fill pot with oasis. Insert floral picks and leaves into oasis.

How-To's continued on page 135

GARDENS OF HISTORIC CHARLESTON
STEWART
Entertaining

Gather oranges, lemons, or limes plus spices to put together fragrant arrangements. Here, gilded orange peels, raffia-tied cinnamon sticks, and nuggets of nutmeg form a wonderfully aromatic wreath.

SPICE WREATH

You need: 18 cinnamon sticks; raffia; gilt wax; 17 dried oranges; glue gun; dried mace; 12" grapevine wreath; 80 pieces of whole nutmeg; 12" of wire.
Assembling: Arrange cinnamon sticks into 6 bundles; tie with raffia. Rub bundles and oranges with gilt wax. Glue mace to wreath. Glue cinnamon bundles, oranges, and nutmeg to wreath.
Finishing: Fold wire in half; twist to make hanging loop. Twist ends around back of wreath.

CULINARY TOPIARY

You need: Terra-cotta pot with smooth sides; cinnamon sticks; low-temp glue gun; 2 plastic foam cones (1 slightly larger than the other); 16-gauge floral wire; star anise; 28-gauge floral wire; whole cloves.
Preparing pot and cones: Glue cinnamon sticks, evenly spaced, to side of pot. Glue small cone into pot. Push four lengths of 16-gauge wire into small cone, then center large cone on top.
Decorating cone: Twist lengths of 28-gauge wire around star anise, then stick wire ends into large cone to secure. Push cloves into large cone, covering remainder of surface.
Finishing: Cross two cinnamon sticks; secure with wire. Wire sticks to top of cone.

CARDAMOM POMANDER

You need: 3" plastic foam ball; whole cloves; green cardamom pods; low-temp glue gun; raffia; floral wire.
Making pomander: Poke cloves into foam ball to divide it into quarters. Glue cardamom pods in between, covering ball.
Finishing: Tie several strands of raffia in a bow. Fold a 6" length of floral wire into a "U" shape. Pin bow to top of ball with wire shape. Knot ends of several loose ends of raffia together to form a hanging loop.

Trim a foam cone with star anise and stud with whole cloves for our culinary topiary (above, from left). *Craft classic cardamom-and-clove pomanders to let spicy scents waft from every window.*

twinkle, twinkle

REFLECT THE RADIANCE OF THE DAY WITH SHIMMERING SILVER, SPARKLING CRYSTAL, THE BRILLIANT BLUES OF A STARLIT SKY. THIS IS DAZZLING ELEGANCE AT ITS EASIEST!

String crystal beads and silver balls onto wire (opposite), *then twist into stars, snowflakes, or any shape that strikes your fancy.* (Below) *Twinkle, twinkle, little tree! Plant a pint-size pine in a gold-banded pail. To adorn, dot white ribbon with a silver glitter pen, then weave it gracefully through the branches. Bedeck the boughs with beaded ornaments, all glimmery and shimmery. Present gifts in star-stamped wraps.*

How-To's on page 136

How-To's on page 136

To ornament a door or window, create a gorgeous star (opposite) flashing with silver balls and silvered pinecones. Trim the tree with accents inspired by the twilit sky (clockwise from top left): Painted Christmas balls begin with wooden spheres purchased from a craft store. For celestial ornaments, cut shapes from blue velvet or satin, stitch and stuff, then tack on a constellation of sequins. Beaded baubles reminiscent of snowflakes and stars gleam among the branches.

How-To's on page 142

Light up the dining room with silvery white accents. Our decorative gingerbread castle is roofed with sugared-cereal squares and trimmed with white icing and silver dragées. Settle your cookie creation on a patch of silver-sprayed burlap for a magical centerpiece. Drape the table with a snowy cloth sewn with gleaming beads; set with your most polished possessions and craft shining silver crackers for each place.

sugar and spice

CANDIES, COOKIES, AND TREATS GALORE — SET THE SCENE FOR FUN WITH THE SWEETEST ACCENTS OF ALL! MAKE USE OF PEPPERMINT STRIPES, GINGERBREAD SHAPES, AND FAVORITE CANDIES FOR DECORATIONS THAT LOOK ALMOST GOOD ENOUGH TO EAT.

Santa at your service! Our wooden butler Claus (right) *can gather gifts or offer refreshments.* (Opposite) *Greet little ones with goodies as they come down the stairs...wrap the banister with red ribbon and evergreens. Hang a quartet of stockings for St. Nick to fill!*

How-To's on page 144

Create a whimsical wonderland to delight the family: Bake up a batch of teddy-shaped cookies (top) *using your favorite recipe; pipe on icing faces and outfits. If they won't be eaten, glue on tiny buttons and ribbon bow ties.* (Bottom) *Let your imagination go with these "present-ations!" Stamp white candy canes on green paper and paint on the details, glue candy canes to wide red ribbon, and use colorful candy dots as ribbon and tie with a gauzy bow.*

TEDDY ORNAMENTS

You need: Gingerbread Dough (see recipe, page 77); large teddy-bear cookie cutter; 1 recipe of Royal Icing (see recipe, page 77); paste food coloring; pastry bag fitted with small round tip; 1/8"W ribbon. *Optional* – Small buttons; ribbon bows; glue gun.

Baking cookies: Following recipe, prepare dough; bake. (For edible ornaments, poke hole in top of each before baking.) Let cool.

Decorating: Divide icing; tint with food coloring as desired. Pipe icing vest or shorts, eyes, nose, and mouth. Let dry. (If to be eaten, tie 10" ribbon through hole to hang.) If not to be eaten, glue on buttons and ribbon bow ties. For hanger, cut a 10" ribbon; curl to form loop; glue to back.

STAR TREE TOPPER

You need: Cardboard; hard candies – barber poles, 1 lollipop, peppermint pillows; glue gun; elastic.

To do: On cardboard, draw a 9"W freehand star. Cut out. Glue barber poles on edges to outline. Cut stick off lollipop; glue to center of star; fill in with peppermint pillows. Glue a piece of elastic to back of star; slip elastic over treetop.

How-To's continued on page 50

Involve the family in making the ornaments for this scrumptious tree. Oversize faux candies are cut from foam and wrapped in cellophane. Bundles of cinnamon sticks and fresh fruit pomanders offer spicy fragrance, and a garland of Battenberg lace gets a frosty finish with glitter. The striking star tree topper is crafted from cardboard and real candies.

Share a yummy Yuletide with drop-in guests. To make our candy topiary (right), *glue wrapped sweets to a foam globe; keep a pair of scissors handy so folks can snip off a treat!* (Opposite) *Charming cookie cottages, "mortared" with icing and trimmed with candies, are sweet additions to the tree.*

CANDY TOPIARY

You need: Terra-cotta pot with 6" dia. opening; red spray paint; acrylic paints – blue, yellow, brown; paintbrushes; 12"H x 1/2" dia. wooden dowel; 4" dia. plastic foam ball; floral foam; low-temp glue gun; wrapped hard candies; straight pins; Spanish moss; 1 1/2 yds of 1/2"W ribbon; small scissors.

Painting pot: Spray pot with red paint; let dry. Paint rim of pot yellow. Freehand paint blue rectangle on pot; add yellow border and stars.

Making topiary: Paint dowel brown; let dry. Glue floral foam into pot. Insert dowel into foam ball, gluing to secure. Insert dowel into foam in pot, gluing to secure. Use straight pins to attach candies to foam ball, covering completely.

Finishing: Cut an 18" length of ribbon; tie one end to scissors handle. Pin other end to topiary. Tie remaining ribbon in bow; pin to topiary. Cover foam in pot with moss; glue to secure.

COOKIE COTTAGE ORNAMENTS

You need: Pastry bag fitted with round tip; Royal Icing (see recipe, page 77); assorted cookies; 6" of 1/4"W ribbon or trim (for each); assorted candies.

Assembling: Fill pastry bag with icing. Arrange cookies to form sides of cottage; pipe icing along cookie edges; hold until icing sets. Attach cookie roof in same way.

Decorating: Fold ribbon in half for hanging loop; secure to roof with icing. Cover roof with thick layer of icing; press candies into icing.

*T*ransform a dining nook with just a few details. (Opposite) *Replace that everyday framed print with a green wreath; dress up a plain tablecloth with a cheerful runner. Fill clear apothecary jars or footed vases with assorted candies to anchor faux amaryllis (for fresh cut flowers, place a water-filled glass in the container and lay candy in around it). Favors in green-sprigged boxes enhance the table.* (This page, top) *Tie jumbo jingle bells to white pine with a bright bow; pin to a corner of the table or hang from a chandelier.* (Bottom) *Tuck a handwritten place card in a chunk of ribbon candy; set on a pretty napkin.*

CANDY ORNAMENTS

You need: *Lollipops* – 2½" dia. plastic foam ball(s) (each ball makes 2 ornaments); serrated knife; toothpicks; bamboo skewers; white tissue paper; decoupage medium. *Mints* – 3¾" dia. x ⅜" thick papier-maché disk. *Both* – Paintbrushes (flat, round); acrylic paint – white, red, fuchsia; dimensional paint – red, pink, pearlescent; satin varnish; clear cellophane wrap; ⅜"W red dotted grosgrain ribbon; scarlet jumbo rickrack; transparent tape.

Preparing lollipops: Cut foam balls in half with serrated knife. Poke in toothpick as temporary handle.

Decoupaging lollipops: With flat brush, cover half-balls with decoupage medium. Tear white tissue into 1"W strips. Glue strips, pressing them into medium. Brush medium over foam as needed, adding strips until covered. Let dry overnight.

Painting lollipops and mints: Paint ornaments and skewers white; let dry. Use a pencil to draw swirls or curved wedge shapes on rounded side of each ornament. Use round brush to paint in areas, alternating red or fuchsia acrylic paint with white. Let dry.

Painting details: Use contrasting-color dimensional paint to outline swirls and draw double lines between wedges. Let dry. Brush with a coat of varnish.

Finishing lollipops: Cut skewers in 8" lengths. Poke a skewer "stick" into each half-ball. Cut cellophane in 12" squares; wrap around lollipop, gathering around skewer at base of lollipop. Tie with ribbon and rickrack.

Finishing mints: Cut a piece of cellophane 8"W x 12"L. Wrap and tape cellophane at back of mint. Twist cellophane ends on either side of mint and secure by tying on ribbon and rickrack bows.

How-To's continued on page 147

PAUL

something for everyone

A TEDDY BEAR FOR A FAVORITE NEPHEW, AN APRON FOR A HOLIDAY COOK, A FANCIFUL BUTTON WREATH FOR YOUR BEST FRIEND...THIS COLLECTION HAS SOMETHING FOR EVERYONE, CRAFTED WITH LOVE BY YOU!

STARRY SCARF AND FANCIFUL HAT

You need: 60"W fleece – 1 yd red, 1/4 yd yellow, scraps of white and green; 12 assorted buttons; 1 yd red ball fringe; embroidery floss – green, yellow.

Making patterns: Enlarge pattern (page 149; 1/2" seam allowances for hat are included). Make patterns using full-sized star patterns (page 148).

Scarf – Cutting fleece: Cut two 8" x 30" pieces – one red, one yellow. Cut eight stars from assorted colors (four large, four small).

Trimming: Pin two stars to each end of scarf pieces; hand-sew with green floss and blanket stitches. Sew a button in center of each. Cut two 8" pieces of fringe and pin to ends of red piece, edges even; stitch.

Finishing: Pin scarf pieces together, right sides facing, fringe inside "sandwich." Stitch (1/2" seam), leaving 4"L opening on one long side. Turn; slipstitch closed.

Hat – Cutting fleece: From red, trace and cut two hat pieces, then fold remaining fleece in half; place brim pattern with dash lines on fold; cut two brims. From remaining colors, cut four stars (two medium, two small).

Stitching: Pin hat pieces together; stitch (1/2" seam); leave bottom open.

How-To's continued on page 148

Whip up these easy-do chill chasers (opposite) in brilliant hues. Whimsical appliqués add punch; for even more fun, the scarf reverses to yellow with red, white, and green stars. (This page, top) Whether you send just one to someone special or cinch together several to give as a friendship token, these keepsake note cards are beautiful enough to frame. (Bottom) Tie up gifts with red or green raffia, twine, or ribbon finished with bells, berry stickers, or a clip-on ladybug ornament.

BUTTON-RICH WREATH

You need: 8" dia. plastic foam wreath; 2½ yds of 1⅞"W taupe wire-edged ribbon; glue gun; about 250 assorted buttons; sprigs of faux greenery; ½ yd of narrow gold trim.

To do: For hanging loop, pass ribbon around wreath once and knot ends to create loop in back. Wrap entire wreath with ribbon, leaving loop exposed. Glue ribbon ends. Save remaining ribbon for bow. Glue buttons to cover front and sides only. Tie remaining ribbon in a bow; glue to top of wreath. Tuck in sprigs; secure with glue. Tie a gold-trim bow around bow/sprigs.

TINY TREE

You need: One hank of green seed beads (size 11); small dish; 1 spool of 32-gauge brass wire (branches); 6" of 18-gauge stiff floral wire (trunk); wire cutters; floral tape; small flowerpot; gold paint; floral foam; jewelry glue; glue gun; ⅞"W gold star charm; ½"W rhinestone circle charm; 55 (total) small charms and ornaments; 55 small gold-tone jump rings: jewelry pliers (round nose and smooth-jawed flat nose).

Tree is constructed from top down; consult diagrams (page 151) often while stringing beads.

Making tree top: Pour some beads in dish. Cut a 10" piece of 32-gauge wire. *First loop* – Slip on 15 beads. Center beads on wire and twist ends against beads, making a loop, ends free. *Second loop* – On one end of one wire slip on 20 beads. Snug beads up against loop. Loop wire, wrapping end between the seventh and eighth beads away from first loop. Pull snug. *Third loop* – Repeat with other end of wire. Next, slip seven beads on each end of wire, then twist together, making a three-loop branch. Now hold the top loop in one hand and the wire ends in the other and turn the whole piece so it twists around itself.

Attaching tree top to trunk: Bend down (⅜") one end of 18-gauge wire. Wrap loose wire ends of beaded tree top around the bent-down end of trunk so bead loops extend above trunk. Set aside.

Making top (first) row of branches: Work from top of tree toward base. Using same technique as tree top, cut five 10"L pieces of wire. On each, slip on 13 beads, centered, and twist ends together against beads. Next, slip six beads on each wire and twist ends together against beads. Wrap ends of the five branches around trunk just below top, evenly spaced.

How-To's continued on page 150

Spread cheer with festive home accents: (Opposite, from left) *Hit the flea markets or dig through your sewing basket to find an assortment of buttons for this one-of-a-kind wreath. Only six inches tall, this intricately beaded tabletop tree is guaranteed to dazzle!* (Below) *Strips of ribbon and trim lend rich color and touchable texture to handsome, simple-to-sew cushions.*

Hide extra-special gifts in these treasure boxes. Metallic paints, colorful fabric scraps, charms, and beads transform ordinary boxes into caches with lots of character. Notice how painted drawer pulls become jazzy handles or feet.

It's clear — glassware makes great gifts! You can personalize any translucent present with a few colorful strokes of a brush. Created with water-based paints, the decorative designs are non-toxic, and with careful handling, your fanciful flourishes will last for many Christmases to come.

SQUARE TREASURE BOX

You need: 7³/₄" x 7³/₄" square kraft-paper box; wood glue; wooden knob; craft/fabric glue; paintbrushes; gesso; metallic acrylic paint – light gold, dark gold, purple, green, red, blue; sea sponge; antiquing medium (mahogany); rag; scraps of felt (assorted colors); 8" x 8" square each of thin white cotton fabric and sheer net; 2¹/₄ yds of 1¹/₂"W metallic gold ribbon; small gold-tone charms; white embroidery floss; assorted glass beads; brown mailing tape.

Adding handle: Glue knob in center of lid with wood glue.

Painting: Prime box and lid with gesso; let dry. Sponge-paint lid and sides of box light gold; let dry. Sponge dark gold on sides of box. Paint lid lip dark gold; when dry, brush on strokes of color for confetti effect. Paint knob green; let dry. With tip of brush handle, dot on light gold. Apply antiquing medium; wipe off excess with rag.

Decorating: *You will be making eight heart patches*. Cut eight 2"L x 1¹/₂"W hearts from assorted felt. Cut eight 2¹/₄" x 2¹/₂" pieces each of cotton and net. Cut eight 2"L pieces of gold ribbon. To make each patch, stack white cotton, ribbon, heart, net; hand-sew layers together with overcast stitches and one strand of floss. Sew beads and charms to hearts as desired. Glue patches to lid (with fabric glue), as shown. Wrap box bottom with ribbons centered vertically on each side; secure ends of ribbon inside box with mailing tape.

ROUND TREASURE BOX

You need: 7¹/₂" dia. x 6"T kraft-paper box; wood glue; 4 small knobs; paintbrushes; sea sponge; gesso; metallic acrylic paint – medium gold, light gold, red, light purple; decoupage medium; red paper; variety of sheer and opaque fabric/ribbons; fabric glue; beads; gold-tone Cupid charm; 4" of gold cord.

Adding feet: Glue knobs to box bottom (at corners) with wood glue.

How-To's continued on page 152

Youngsters can paint jingle bells with frosty faces to make a slew of snowman necklaces for their friends — great for party favors! Our easy-to-make marionette lets pint-size puppeteers put on a show. Scraps of dowels, fabric, yarn, and string will get him dancing in no time. (Opposite) Just the right size for hugging, the teddy bear toy and stuffed Scottie dog are shaped from holly-red felt and boiled wool and simply sewn with blanket stitches.

SNOWMAN NECKLACES

You need: 33mm jingle bells; small paintbrush; white acrylic paint; 1/8" hole punch; craft foam – black, orange; craft glue; 1/4" green pom-poms; white floral wire; glue gun; red yarn.

Making snowmen: Paint bells white; let dry. For each snowman, punch seven circles from black foam and cut 3/8"L triangle from orange foam for nose. Holding each bell upside down, use craft glue to attach two circles to bell for eyes, five circles to bell for mouth, and nose between eyes and mouth; let dry. Cut 2 1/2" piece of wire; bend into half-circle. Hot-glue wire ends to sides of bell for top of ear muffs. Glue pom-pom over each end of wire. Cut a length of yarn for necklace; fold in half. Knot ends together. Slip folded end under hanging loop of bell; pull knotted ends through fold to attach necklace.

How-To's continued on page 154

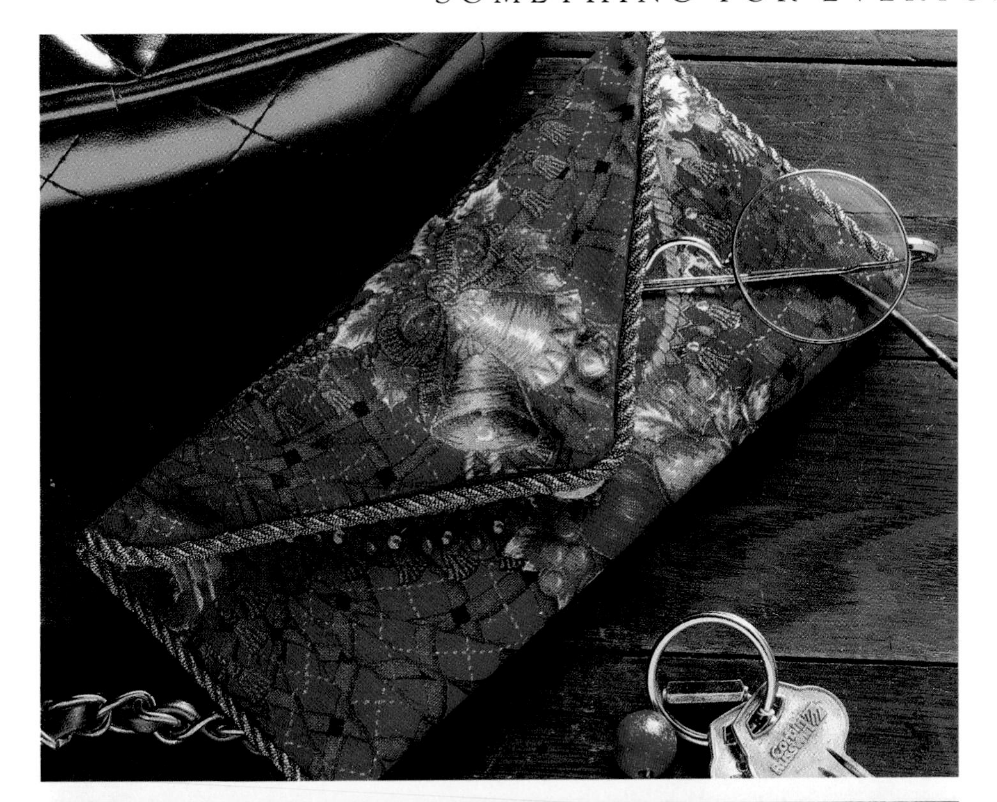

His-and-her vests (opposite) *use a standard pattern in vibrant fabrics. Dress up one with embossed gold buttons, the other with jeweled fasteners.* (Left) *Our brocade eyeglass case is a practical present, elegantly executed. Pad with soft fabric to protect the specs.* (Below) *What nifty mittens! For a playful touch, do stripes on one, polka-dots on the other.*

NIFTY MITTENS

Sizes: Adult S/M, M/L.
You need: Worsted weight yarn (100 gr/247 yds per skein) – 1 each red (R), gold (G); set of 4 dp needles, size 8; stitch holder; yarn needle.
Gauge: 18 sts = 4"; 24 rows = 4".
Note: Left and right mittens are shaped in same way. Instructions are given for smaller size. Changes for larger size are given in parentheses. If only 1 number is given, it applies to both sizes.

Striped Mitten

Pattern: K 3 rnds G, K 3 rnds R. With R, cast on 36 (44) sts, divided evenly on 3 needles. Work in k2p2 ribbing for 2 (2½)". ***First rnd:*** Work in St st. Inc 2 (0) sts evenly spaced – 38 (44) sts. Change to G; beg patt; at same time, inc 1 at beg of 6th rnd to beg thumb shaping. ***Next rnd:*** K all sts – 39 (45) sts. ***Next rnd:*** Inc 1, K1, inc 1, K across. ***Next rnd:*** K all sts. ***Next rnd:*** Inc 1, K3, inc 1, K across. ***Next rnd:*** K all sts. Continue as established, inc at beg of rnd with 2 more sts between incs every other row 3 times, then every 3rd rnd 0 (1) time – 49 (57) sts.

How-To's continued on page 152

Youngsters can paint jingle bells with frosty faces to make a slew of snowman necklaces for their friends — great for party favors! Our easy-to-make marionette lets pint-size puppeteers put on a show. Scraps of dowels, fabric, yarn, and string will get him dancing in no time. (Opposite) *Just the right size for hugging, the teddy bear toy and stuffed Scottie dog are shaped from holly-red felt and boiled wool and simply sewn with blanket stitches.*

SNOWMAN NECKLACES

You need: 33mm jingle bells; small paintbrush; white acrylic paint; 1/8" hole punch; craft foam – black, orange; craft glue; 1/4" green pom-poms; white floral wire; glue gun; red yarn.

Making snowmen: Paint bells white; let dry. For each snowman, punch seven circles from black foam and cut 3/8"L triangle from orange foam for nose. Holding each bell upside down, use craft glue to attach two circles to bell for eyes, five circles to bell for mouth, and nose between eyes and mouth; let dry. Cut 2 1/2" piece of wire; bend into half-circle. Hot-glue wire ends to sides of bell for top of ear muffs. Glue pom-pom over each end of wire. Cut a length of yarn for necklace; fold in half. Knot ends together. Slip folded end under hanging loop of bell; pull knotted ends through fold to attach necklace.

How-To's continued on page 154

It's clear — glassware makes great gifts! You can personalize any translucent present with a few colorful strokes of a brush. Created with water-based paints, the decorative designs are non-toxic, and with careful handling, your fanciful flourishes will last for many Christmases to come.

SQUARE TREASURE BOX

You need: 7¾" x 7¾" square kraft-paper box; wood glue; wooden knob; craft/fabric glue; paintbrushes; gesso; metallic acrylic paint – light gold, dark gold, purple, green, red, blue; sea sponge; antiquing medium (mahogany); rag; scraps of felt (assorted colors); 8" x 8" square each of thin white cotton fabric and sheer net; 2¼ yds of 1½"W metallic gold ribbon; small gold-tone charms; white embroidery floss; assorted glass beads; brown mailing tape.

Adding handle: Glue knob in center of lid with wood glue.

Painting: Prime box and lid with gesso; let dry. Sponge-paint lid and sides of box light gold; let dry. Sponge dark gold on sides of box. Paint lid lip dark gold; when dry, brush on strokes of color for confetti effect. Paint knob green; let dry. With tip of brush handle, dot on light gold. Apply antiquing medium; wipe off excess with rag.

Decorating: *You will be making eight heart patches*. Cut eight 2"L x 1½"W hearts from assorted felt. Cut eight 2¼" x 2½" pieces each of cotton and net. Cut eight 2"L pieces of gold ribbon. To make each patch, stack white cotton, ribbon, heart, net; hand-sew layers together with overcast stitches and one strand of floss. Sew beads and charms to hearts as desired. Glue patches to lid (with fabric glue), as shown. Wrap box bottom with ribbons centered vertically on each side; secure ends of ribbon inside box with mailing tape.

ROUND TREASURE BOX

You need: 7½" dia. x 6"T kraft-paper box; wood glue; 4 small knobs; paintbrushes; sea sponge; gesso; metallic acrylic paint – medium gold, light gold, red, light purple; decoupage medium; red paper; variety of sheer and opaque fabric/ribbons; fabric glue; beads; gold-tone Cupid charm; 4" of gold cord.

Adding feet: Glue knobs to box bottom (at corners) with wood glue.

How-To's continued on page 152

HOST AND HOSTESS VESTS

You need: Desired vest sewing pattern; 1/2 yd each of 3 different fabrics (silk print for front, silk solid for back, and solid lining fabric); decorative buttons or fasteners.
Making vests: Follow pattern instructions to cut and sew vest. Make buttonholes large enough to accommodate buttons; stitch buttons to front edge of vest.

BROCADE EYEGLASS CASE

You need: Christmas-print fabric; lining fabric; large snap; gold cord trim.
Making pattern: Determine desired finished length and width of case and draw this shape on paper. At lower edge, add finished length to this shape for front of case. At upper edge, draw desired flap shape. Add 1/2" to pattern all around.
Cutting: Using pattern, cut one piece of print fabric and one piece of lining.
Assembling: Pin case to lining, with right sides facing and raw edges even. Stitch in 1/2" seams, leaving opening on one edge for turning. Turn; press. Slipstitch opening closed. Fold up front of case, right side out. Slipstitch side edges. Sew half of snap to wrong side of flap near point. Fold down flap; sew other half of snap to right side of front, under hook section.
Finishing: Slipstitch cord along all edges.

GIFTS of FLAVOR

GOOD THINGS COME IN SMALL PACKAGES! TO PRESENT FLAVORFUL OFFERINGS FROM YOUR KITCHEN, KEEP AN EYE OUT FOR DECORATIVE BASKETS, BOTTLES, TINS, AND CANISTERS ALL YEAR LONG. THE CONTAINERS BECOME GIFTS IN THEMSELVES!

White and dark Chocolate-Dipped Pretzels (opposite) *team sweet and salty deliciously. A subtle touch of syrup enriches Maple-Nut Rugelach* (this page). *If you like, substitute almonds or pecans for the walnuts rolled into these crisp cookie crescents.*

CHOCOLATE-DIPPED PRETZELS

- **5 ounces semisweet chocolate chips**
- **5 ounces small pretzels, each about 1 1/2 inches in diameter**
- **5 ounces white chocolate squares, for baking**
- **Colored sprinkles, for decoration**

1. Melt semisweet chocolate according to package directions; place in small bowl. Line baking sheets with waxed paper.
2. Dip half of pretzels, 1 at a time, in semisweet chocolate. Using 2-pronged kitchen fork, tap off excess chocolate over bowl; place coated pretzels on waxed paper. If chocolate begins to thicken, reheat briefly for easier coating.
3. Repeat process with white chocolate and remaining pretzels.
4. To decorate, sprinkle some of pretzels with colored sprinkles.
5. To drizzle chocolate, spoon leftover melted chocolate into small square-cornered (nonpleated) plastic bags, pushing chocolate into 1 corner. Snip off very end of corner and use like a pastry bag, drizzling either of 2 chocolates on remaining coated pretzels (white chocolate on dark pretzels, dark chocolate on white pretzels). Let cool at room temperature until chocolate is set. Store in cool place, layered between sheets of waxed paper, in airtight containers.
Yield: Makes about 100 pieces.

MAPLE-NUT RUGELACH

Dough:
- **4 ounces (half 8-ounce package) cream cheese, softened**
- **1/3 cup unsalted butter**
- **1/4 cup sugar**
- **2 tablespoons maple syrup**
- **1/4 teaspoon salt**
- **1 egg yolk**
- **1 1/2 cups all-purpose flour**

Filling:
- **1 cup finely ground walnuts**
- **1/3 cup sugar**
- **2 tablespoons maple syrup**
- **1/8 teaspoon ground cinnamon**

Glaze:
- **1 egg white**
- **1 teaspoon water**
- **1 teaspoon sugar**

1. Prepare Dough: In large bowl, beat cream cheese, butter, 1/4 cup sugar, 2 tablespoons maple syrup, salt, and egg yolk until smooth. Beat in flour just until blended. Shape dough into ball. Refrigerate until firm, about 2 hours.
2. Prepare Filling: In medium-size bowl, stir walnuts, 1/3 cup sugar, 2 tablespoons maple syrup, and cinnamon.
3. Heat oven to 350°. Grease 2 baking sheets.
4. Divide dough in half. On lightly floured surface, with floured rolling pin, roll out half of dough to 1/8-inch thickness. Cut into 10-inch circle. Spread circle with half of walnut mixture; cut into 16 wedges. Starting with wide edge, roll up each wedge, jelly-roll fashion. Place cookies, wedge point down, on baking sheets. Repeat with remaining dough and filling.
5. Prepare Glaze: Lightly beat egg white with water; brush over cookies. Sprinkle with 1 teaspoon sugar.
6. Bake in 350° oven for 15 to 20 minutes or until lightly browned. Remove from baking sheets to wire racks to cool.
Yield: Makes about 32 cookies.

30-MINUTE VEGETABLE PICKLES

These crisp veggies are not processed, so be sure to keep them refrigerated.

- 6 carrots, diagonally sliced
- 3 cups small cauliflower florets
- 2 large sweet red peppers
- 2 large zucchini
- 1 cup brine-packed whole green olives
- 3 cups water
- 3 cups distilled white vinegar
- 2 teaspoons Italian seasoning
- 1 teaspoon garlic powder
- 2 teaspoons sugar
- 2 teaspoons crushed red-pepper flakes

1. In large saucepan, bring enough water to cover carrots and cauliflower to a boil. Add carrots and cauliflower; cook 3 minutes; drain. Cut peppers and zucchini into 1/4 x 1/4 x 2-inch strips.
2. Divide olives between 6 pint-size wide-mouth jars (see Note). Add cauliflower in one layer, then stand red-pepper and zucchini sticks on top of cauliflower; top with carrots.
3. Combine 3 cups water, vinegar, Italian seasoning, garlic powder, sugar, and red-pepper flakes in medium saucepan. Bring to boiling; boil 1 minute.
4. Pour hot-vinegar mixture over vegetables in jars, making sure vegetables are covered in each jar. Screw on lids tightly. Refrigerate at least 1 day for flavors to develop. Pickles can be stored up to 3 weeks in refrigerator.
Yield: Makes 6 pint jars.
Note: If you wish, arrange vegetables in two 1 1/2-quart glass containers, as pictured.

Friends will adore Smoky Sam's BBQ Sauce (top), a terrific tomato-vinegar blend. Artfully arrange crisp, tangy 30-Minute Vegetable Pickles (bottom) in generous jars. (Opposite) Our fragrant Gingerbraid wreath can stand in as a centerpiece.

SMOKY SAM'S BBQ SAUCE

- 1/4 cup peanut oil
- 2 large onions, finely chopped (2 cups)
- 4 cloves garlic, finely chopped
- 2 cans (28 ounces each) crushed tomatoes
- 1 1/4 cups cider vinegar
- 6 tablespoons firmly packed dark-brown sugar
- 3 tablespoons Worcestershire sauce
- 2 tablespoons ground black pepper
- 2 tablespoons chili powder
- 1 tablespoon salt
- 2 teaspoons liquid smoke
- 1 teaspoon ground cumin
- 1/2 teaspoon ground red pepper, or to taste

1. Heat oil in large, heavy nonaluminum saucepan over medium heat. Add the onion and garlic; sauté for 5 minutes or until the onion is softened.
2. Stir in the tomatoes, vinegar, brown sugar, Worcestershire sauce, black pepper, chili powder, salt, liquid smoke, cumin, and red pepper until well blended. Bring to boiling. Reduce the heat; simmer, uncovered, for 2 hours or until the mixture is thickened, stirring occasionally. Toward the end of cooking, make sure to stir frequently so that the sauce doesn't scorch on the bottom of the saucepan.
3. Let the sauce cool slightly. Working in batches, spoon the sauce mixture into a blender or food processor. Whirl until puréed.
4. Transfer the sauce to a container with a tight-fitting lid. Let cool completely, uncovered. Then seal tightly.
5. Refrigerate the sauce for up to 2 weeks. Use in your favorite rib or grilled chicken recipe or spoon over burgers, hot dogs, or grilled fish.
Yield: Makes 6 cups.

GINGERBRAID

Dough:

- **2 envelopes active dry yeast**
- **1 cup warm water (105° to 115°)**
- **½ cup (1 stick) butter, at room temperature**
- **3 tablespoons sugar**
- **2 eggs**
- **⅓ cup dark molasses**
- **3 tablespoons ground ginger**
- **2 tablespoons finely chopped crystallized ginger**
- **¾ teaspoon ground cinnamon**
- **1 teaspoon salt**
- **½ teaspoon ground black pepper**
- **4 cups bread flour**

Glaze:

- **¼ cup sugar**
- **2 tablespoons water**

1. Prepare Dough: Sprinkle yeast over warm water in small bowl. Let stand until foamy, about 5 minutes.
2. Beat butter in large bowl until creamy. Beat in sugar until fluffy. Beat in eggs. On low speed, beat in molasses, ground ginger, half the crystallized ginger, cinnamon, salt, pepper, and 2 cups bread flour. On low speed, beat in yeast mixture and ⅓ cup flour until smooth.
3. Stir in some of remaining flour. Continue adding flour until dough is workable with hands without sticking. Use any remaining flour to dust work surface. Knead dough until soft and elastic, about 5 minutes. Transfer to large greased bowl, turning to coat. Cover with clean towel. Let rise in warm place until doubled in volume, about 2 hours.
4. Coat 9½ x 4-inch tube pan with nonstick vegetable-oil cooking spray. Punch down dough. Divide dough into 3 equal pieces. Using hands, roll each piece into 22-inch-long rope. Place ropes side by side, touching. Gently press one end of each rope onto work surface. This is "top" of braid. Begin braiding ropes, by lifting left rope across and over middle rope. Next, take right rope and lift it across and over new middle rope.

Continue alternating sides, always lifting outside rope across and over middle rope, gently tugging on ropes to stretch slightly. Gently form braid into ring; press ends of ring together, sealing with a little water. Transfer to prepared tube pan. Cover with cloth. Let rise in warm place until doubled in volume, 45 to 60 minutes.
5. Heat oven to 350°. Bake risen braid for about 35 minutes or until puffed and lightly browned. Remove inner section of tube pan, then remove bread to rack; you may need to run a knife around edges of pan if it sticks.
6. Prepare Glaze: While bread cools, heat sugar and water in small saucepan over medium heat until sugar is completely dissolved. Let syrup cool slightly. Brush over top of braid. Sprinkle with remaining tablespoon chopped crystallized ginger. Serve warm or at room temperature.
Yield: Makes 16 servings.

CHOCOLATE-DIPPED SPOONS

Melt separately, according to package directions, 4 squares (1 ounce each) bittersweet OR semisweet chocolate, chopped, and 4 squares (1 ounce each) premium white chocolate, chopped. Line baking sheets with waxed paper. Dip metal or heavy-weight decorative plastic teaspoons into chocolate; place on waxed paper to cool. Let sit until chocolate hardens, about 1 hour. For two-toned spoons, redip in alternate chocolate. Place in airtight container between sheets of waxed paper; store in cool place up to 3 weeks.

Yield: Coats about 24 spoons.

Chocolate-Dipped Spoons (this page, from left) *will let coffee lovers enjoy a mocha flavor as they stir their favorite brew. You can whip up a batch of rich Chocolate Pecans on your stovetop in no time. Present them in elegant ribbon bags* (see instructions, page 155).

CHOCOLATE PECANS

- **1 package (12 ounces) butterscotch chips**
- **1 package (10 ounces) peanut-butter chips**
- **1 package (6 ounces) semisweet chocolate chips**
- **6 ounces chocolate candy coating**
- **2 cups chopped pecans, toasted**

1. Line a baking sheet with lightly greased waxed paper.

2. Stirring constantly, melt butterscotch chips, peanut-butter chips, chocolate chips, and candy coating in a heavy large saucepan over low heat. Stir in pecans.

3. Drop mixture by tablespoonfuls onto the prepared baking sheet. Set candies aside to harden.

4. Store in airtight container in a cool place until ready to pack the ribbon bags.

Yield: Makes about 70 candies.

CANDIED WALNUTS

- **3/4 cup firmly packed light-brown sugar**
- **2 tablespoons orange juice**
- **1 teaspoon grated orange zest**
- **1/2 teaspoon salt**
- **1 pound walnut halves**

1. Heat oven to 350° (microwave directions follow).

2. Combine brown sugar, orange juice, zest, and salt in large bowl. Add walnuts; toss to coat. Line large jelly-roll pan with aluminum foil. Coat with nonstick vegetable-oil cooking spray. Spread walnut mixture evenly over foil.

3. Bake nut mixture in 350° oven 20 to 25 minutes or until dark brown and bubbly, stirring halfway through cooking time.

4. Meanwhile, coat large piece of foil with nonstick vegetable-oil cooking spray. Remove nut mixture from oven. Immediately spread on prepared foil, separating nuts with 2 forks. Cool completely. Store in airtight container for up to 3 weeks.

Microwave Directions: Coat walnuts as in Step 2, then cook in large microwave-safe glass baking dish on full (100%) power for 8 to 10 minutes, stirring every 2 minutes, until dark brown and bubbly. Proceed with Step 4.

Yield: Makes about 4 1/2 cups.

CHILI CASHEWS

- 1 egg white
- 3/4 pound unsalted cashews
- 2 tablespoons coarse (kosher) salt
- 1 teaspoon sugar
- 1 teaspoon crushed red-pepper flakes
- 1/2 teaspoon ground cumin
- 1/2 teaspoon leaf oregano, crumbled
- 1/4 teaspoon ground hot red pepper

1. Heat oven to 300°. Lightly beat egg white in medium bowl. Add cashews; toss gently to coat.
2. Combine salt, sugar, red-pepper flakes, cumin, oregano, and ground red pepper. Sprinkle over nut mixture; toss to coat. Spread on greased jelly-roll pan.
3. Bake in 300° oven for 25 minutes or until golden and fragrant, stirring 2 or 3 times during cooking to separate nuts. Cool completely. Store in airtight container at room temperature up to 1 week.
Yield: Makes 12 servings.

TANDOORI-FLAVORED PECANS AND WALNUTS

- 1/2 cup low-fat plain yogurt
- 1/4 cup (1/2 stick) butter or margarine, melted
- 3 tablespoons ground curry powder
- 2 tablespoons ground cumin
- 2 teaspoons salt
- 1 1/2 teaspoons ground cardamom
- 3/4 teaspoon ground hot red pepper
- 1/2 teaspoon sugar
- 1/2 pound pecan halves
- 1/2 pound walnut halves

1. Heat oven to 275°.
2. Combine yogurt, butter, curry, cumin, salt, cardamom, ground red pepper, and sugar in large bowl. Add pecans and walnuts; toss to mix. Spread out nuts in large shallow baking pan.
3. Bake, uncovered, in 275° oven, stirring occasionally, 1 hour or until nuts are golden.
4. Cool completely; store nuts in airtight container up to 3 weeks.
Yield: Makes 4 3/4 cups.

Go nuts with this savory selection: citrusy Candied Walnuts, peppery Chili Cashews, and Tandoori-Flavored Pecans and Walnuts with a curried yogurt coating.

PEANUT BARS

- 1¼ cups all-purpose flour
- ½ teaspoon baking powder
- ½ teaspoon salt
- ¾ cup chopped unsalted peanuts
- ½ cup (1 stick) unsalted butter, at room temperature
- 1 cup sugar
- ¾ cup creamy peanut butter
- 2 eggs
- ⅓ cup corn syrup
- 1 teaspoon vanilla
- Topping or Frosting (recipes, page 69)
- Sprinkles or Drizzle (recipes, page 69)

1. Heat oven to 350°. Line 13 x 9 x 2-inch pan with foil. Coat foil with nonstick vegetable-oil cooking spray.
2. Combine flour, baking powder, salt, and chopped peanuts in bowl.
3. Beat together butter and sugar in large bowl at medium speed until smooth. Beat in peanut butter and eggs until light and creamy. Beat in corn syrup and vanilla until blended. On low speed, beat in flour mixture just until combined. Scrape into prepared pan, spreading level.
4. Bake in 350° oven for 30 to 35 minutes or until wooden pick inserted in center comes out clean. Cool in pan on wire rack 20 minutes.
5. Spread with topping or frosting; decorate with sprinkles or drizzle. Cut into bars.
Yield: Makes 24 bars.

LEMON SHORTBREADS

- ¾ cup toasted almonds
- 1 cup confectioners' sugar
- 1 cup (2 sticks) unsalted butter, at room temperature
- 1 tablespoon grated lemon zest
- 2 egg yolks
- ½ cup cornstarch
- ½ teaspoon salt
- 2 cups all-purpose flour
- Topping or Frosting (recipes, page 69)
- Sprinkles or Drizzle (recipes, page 69)

1. Heat oven to 325°. Line 13 x 9 x 2-inch pan with foil. Coat foil with nonstick vegetable-oil cooking spray.
2. Place almonds and confectioners' sugar in food processor or blender. Whirl until mixture is texture of fine meal.
3. Beat together butter and zest in large bowl until creamy. Beat in yolks, sugar mixture, cornstarch, and salt until smooth and creamy.
4. On low speed, beat in flour just until blended. Scrape into prepared pan, spreading level and pressing to compact.
5. Bake in 325° oven for 25 to 30 minutes or until golden brown. Cool in pan on wire rack 20 minutes.
6. Spread with topping or frosting; decorate with sprinkles or drizzle. Cut into bars.
Yield: Makes 24 bars.

BROWNIE BARS

- 3 squares (1 ounce each) unsweetened chocolate
- ½ cup (1 stick) unsalted butter
- 1 teaspoon instant-coffee crystals
- 1¼ cups sugar
- 2 eggs
- ⅓ cup milk
- 1 teaspoon vanilla
- ¼ teaspoon salt
- 1 cup all-purpose flour
- 1 cup chopped walnuts, about 4 ounces (optional)
- Topping or Frosting (recipes, page 69)
- Sprinkles or Drizzle (recipes, page 69)

1. Heat oven to 350°. Line 13 x 9 x 2-inch pan with foil. Coat foil with nonstick vegetable-oil cooking spray.
2. Melt chocolate and butter in heavy medium saucepan over low heat. Remove pan from heat. Stir in coffee crystals and

sugar. Stir in eggs, milk, vanilla, and salt until well blended. Stir in flour; stir in nuts, if using. Spread mixture evenly in prepared pan.
3. Bake in 350° oven for 22 minutes. Cool in pan on wire rack 30 minutes.
4. Spread with topping or frosting; decorate with sprinkles or drizzle. Cut into bars.
Yield: Makes 24 bars.

TOPPINGS AND FROSTING

Coconut Topping

- **1/2 cup confectioners' sugar**
- **1 tablespoon cornstarch**
- **1 cup half-and-half**
- **1 1/3 cups shredded unsweetened coconut, toasted**
- **1 cup (4 ounces) toasted pecans, coarsely chopped**

Stir together confectioners' sugar, cornstarch, and half-and-half in saucepan until blended. Simmer over medium heat, stirring constantly; cook 1 minute or until thick. Remove from heat. Stir in coconut and pecans. Cool 15 minutes.
Yield: Makes about 2 cups.

Raspberry Topping

- **1 cup cranberry-raspberry juice**
- **1/4 cup cornstarch**
- **1 cup seedless raspberry jam**

Stir together juice and cornstarch in saucepan until blended. Stir in jam. Simmer, stirring occasionally, until thick. Cool 20 minutes.
Yield: Makes about 2 cups.

Milk-Chocolate Frosting

- **1 package (12 ounces) milk-chocolate chips**
- **1/4 cup (1/2 stick) butter, at room temperature, cut into pieces**

Melt chocolate in saucepan over very low heat. Or in microwave-safe container, microwave chocolate at full (100%) power for 2 1/2 to 3 minutes or until melted; stir halfway during cooking time. Stir in butter until smooth.
Yield: Makes about 2 cups.

SPRINKLES AND DRIZZLES

Peanut-Brittle Sprinkles

Place peanut brittle in plastic bag. Crush with rolling pin. Sprinkle over topping or frosting on bar cookies.

Dark-Chocolate Drizzle

Melt 1/3 cup semisweet chocolate chips in saucepan over very low heat. Or melt in microwave-safe container at full (100%) power for 1 to 1 1/2 minutes. Drizzle over topping or frosting on bar cookies.

White-Chocolate Drizzle

Melt together 3 ounces white-chocolate chips and 1 teaspoon vegetable oil in small saucepan over very low heat. Or melt together chocolate and oil in microwave-safe container at full (100%) power for about 1 1/2 minutes, stirring until smooth. Spoon chocolate mixture into small plastic bag, squeezing to 1 corner. Snip off corner; drizzle over topping or frosting on bar cookies.

3 SPICE RUBS

Marrakech:

- **3 tablespoons paprika**
- **1 tablespoon garlic powder**
- **1 tablespoon ground cumin**
- **1 tablespoon ground ginger**
- **2 teaspoons salt**
- **1 1/2 teaspoons ground cinnamon**
- **1 teaspoon ground red pepper**

Santa Fe:

- **3 tablespoons chili powder**
- **1 tablespoon ground cumin**
- **1 tablespoon celery salt**
- **1 tablespoon black pepper**
- **1 1/2 teaspoons garlic salt**
- **1 1/2 teaspoons dried leaf oregano, crumbled**

Spanish Town:

- **2 tablespoons curry powder**
- **1 tablespoon sugar**
- **1 tablespoon ground black pepper**
- **1 tablespoon dried leaf thyme, crumbled**
- **1 tablespoon onion salt**
- **2 teaspoons garlic salt**
- **1 teaspoon ground red pepper**

For each rub, mix all the ingredients in small bowl. Place in jar with tight-fitting lid. Store in cool, dark, dry place for up to 1 year.
To use: Rub **Marrakech** spice mixture over chicken cutlets or pork chops that have been lightly coated with oil or nonstick vegetable-oil cooking spray. Use about 1 tablespoon of rub per pound of cutlets or chops, more or less to suit taste. The **Santa Fe** blend is delicious in any ground beef destined to become hamburgers, meat loaf, and meatballs; use about 2 teaspoons of rub per pound of ground meat. The curry-based **Spanish Town** marries well with chicken, beef, and pork. Rub the mixture over a boneless, rolled pork loin before grilling or roasting, or brighten the taste of chicken or beef stew by adding a teaspoon or two of the spice to onions or other vegetables being sautéed.
Yield: Makes about 1/2 cup of each mix.

Give small rewards like coconut-topped Brownie Bars (opposite), *chocolate-frosted Peanut Bars with peanut-brittle sprinkles, or raspberry-sauced Lemon Shortbreads with white-chocolate drizzle. For friends with a taste for savory treats, our* 3 Spice Rubs (this page) *add zing to meat and poultry.*

CRANBERRY-HONEY JELLY

To wrap, cover lid with a colorful piece of cloth tied on with holiday ribbon.

- **2¼ cups honey**
- **½ cup white corn syrup**
- **¾ cup cranberry juice**
- **3 tablespoons lemon juice**
- **1 pouch (3 ounces) liquid pectin**

1. Mix honey, corn syrup, cranberry juice, and lemon juice in large saucepan. Bring to full rolling boil over medium-high heat, stirring constantly. Quickly pour in pectin. Bring to full rolling boil; boil 1 minute, stirring constantly. Remove from heat.
2. As soon as foam on top becomes a film, skim off film. Pour hot jelly into jars. Screw on lids tightly. Cool and store in refrigerator.
Yield: Makes 4 cups.

LIME CURD

Give this tasty blend as a spread for scones or use as a filling for tartlets or cakes.

- **1¼ cups sugar**
- **½ cup fresh lime juice**
- **2 eggs**
- **4 egg yolks**
- **2 teaspoons fresh grated gingerroot**
- **½ cup (1 stick) unsalted butter; cut into pieces**
- **2 teaspoons grated lime zest**
- **1 drop green liquid food coloring (optional)**

1. Whisk together sugar, lime juice, eggs, egg yolks, and grated gingerroot in medium saucepan. Whisk over medium-low heat, whisking constantly until smooth and mixture begins to thicken, about 15 minutes.
2. Add butter. Whisk until very thick, about 6 minutes. Stir in zest; stir in food coloring, if you wish. Pour into 4-ounce jars or small decorative containers.
3. Cover with lids; refrigerate until cold. (If covering with plastic wrap, press wrap onto surface to prevent skin from forming.) Refrigerate up to 2 weeks.
Yield: Makes 2½ cups.

CHEDDAR-PEPPER STRAWS

- **2 ounces finely shredded Cheddar cheese**
- **2 tablespoons butter, melted**
- **1½ teaspoons cracked black pepper**
- **¾ teaspoon celery salt**
- **1 sheet (½ of 17.3-ounce package) frozen puff pastry, thawed following package directions**
- **1 egg**
- **1 tablespoon water**

1. Heat oven to 400°. Coat 2 large baking sheets with nonstick vegetable-oil cooking spray.
2. Stir together cheese, butter, pepper, and celery salt in a bowl.
3. Unfold pastry on lightly floured surface. Roll into 14 x 10-inch rectangle. With a sharp knife, cut pastry in half lengthwise, pressing straight down through pastry without dragging, to make two 14 x 5-inch rectangles. Cover 1 rectangle with cheese mixture. Place other half of pastry on top of cheese-covered pastry. Roll with rolling pin to seal and flatten.
4. Cut pastry crosswise into twenty-eight ½-inch-wide strips, 5 inches long. Twist each strip; place 1 inch apart on prepared sheets; press ends to seal.
5. Beat egg and water in small bowl. Brush twists with egg mixture.
6. Bake in 400° oven for 10 minutes. Lower heat to 300 °. Bake for 8 to 10 minutes or until golden and crisp. Remove straws to rack to cool.
7. Store in airtight container up to 2 weeks.
Yield: Makes 28 straws.

Cranberry-Honey Jelly and Lime Curd (this page, top) *sweeten breakfast breads or tea cakes. Bring a basket of Cheddar-Pepper Straws* (bottom) — *a welcome hostess gift.* (Opposite) *These tiny treasures, Marzipan Mushrooms and almond-studded Marzipan Pinecones, will melt in your mouth.*

MARZIPAN MUSHROOMS

1 container (8 ounces) almond paste
1 cup confectioners' sugar
1½ tablespoons light corn syrup plus additional for assembling
⅓ cup chocolate chips, melted
Colored nonpareils, for decoration

1. Break almond paste into ½-inch pieces. Place in food processor, along with confectioners' sugar. Process until mixture is the texture of coarse meal.
2. Add corn syrup; process until blended. Test with tablespoon of mixture, rolling into ball between palms. If mixture is crumbly, add additional corn syrup, by teaspoonfuls, just until mixture holds together.
3. Divide marzipan in half. Shape half into small balls of varied sizes, using about ½ teaspoon of the mixture. Flatten on 1 side to shape mushroom caps. Make small indentation in center of flat side to insert stem.
4. With other half of the marzipan, make stems. Roll small balls of marzipan (about scant ½ teaspoon) into oblong shapes.
5. Dip base of each mushroom stem into chocolate, drizzling some down sides. Place on waxed paper until chocolate has hardened. Brush caps with melted chocolate using small brush or palate knife. Sprinkle on decorations; place caps on waxed paper and let stand until chocolate hardens.
6. Dip tip of each mushroom stem into corn syrup and attach to a mushroom cap. Let stand until hardened.
Yield: Makes about 2 dozen.

MARZIPAN PINECONES

1 can (8 ounces) almond paste
Egg-white powder
1⅔ cups confectioners' sugar
Blanched sliced almonds, toasted (see Note)
Light corn syrup, for assembling

1. In medium bowl, break almond paste into small pieces. Knead to make pliable.
2. Follow package directions to mix egg-white powder and water to equal one egg white. Gradually knead confectioners' sugar into almond paste, alternating with egg white mixture, a bit at a time.
3. To form each pinecone: With palms of hands, shape 1 scant tablespoon marzipan into cone shape, about 1½ inches long (rounded at 1 end, pointed at other end).
4. Starting at pointed end of cone and dipping tip of each almond in corn syrup, press almond slices, pointed side in, into marzipan at slight angle and overlapping one another, in rows. Cover cone completely. Store in airtight containers; refrigerate.
Note: To toast almonds, place in single layer in baking pan. Bake in 350° oven 10 minutes or until lightly golden, stirring frequently.
Yield: Makes about 28 pinecones.

tempting TIDBITS

LIGHT THE CANDLES, LET THE CAROLS SOFTLY PLAY... IT'S THE PERFECT EVENING FOR A FESTIVE GATHERING OF FRIENDS. IF EVER NIBBLES SHOULD BE WELCOME, IT'S NOW!

Each of these dips has a skinny secret! Low-fat plain yogurt subs for sour cream in *Spinach-Feta Cheese Dip* (clockwise from bottom left); *Salsa Fresca*, seasoned with lime juice and garlic, is virtually fat-free; and low-cal veggies give *Roasted Red-Pepper Dip* snap. (Opposite) *Caviar Cream Puffs* will go fast.

SALSA FRESCA

- 1 pound plum tomatoes
- 1/2 small red onion, finely chopped
- 1 clove garlic, chopped
- 2 tablespoons fresh lime juice
- 1 tablespoon chopped cilantro
- 1 teaspoon chopped pickled jalapeño pepper, seeded OR 3 dashes hot-pepper sauce
- 1/4 teaspoon salt

1. Core tomatoes; chop. Drain in colander over bowl.
2. Combine tomato with onion, garlic, lime juice, cilantro, jalapeño, and salt. Let stand 2 hours to blend flavors. (Can be made a day ahead and refrigerated, covered.)
Yield: Makes 2 cups.

SPINACH-FETA CHEESE DIP

- 2 cups low-fat plain yogurt
- 1 small clove garlic
- 2 tablespoons chopped fresh dill OR 2 teaspoons dried dill
- 1 package (9 or 10 ounces) frozen leaf spinach, thawed according to package directions, excess liquid squeezed out
- 4 ounces feta cheese, cut into cubes
- 1 teaspoon grated lemon zest
- 1/4 teaspoon salt
- 1/4 teaspoon ground black pepper

1. Set coffee filter or double thickness of paper toweling in strainer over small bowl. Spoon yogurt into filter. Refrigerate; drain for 2 hours. (Yield is about 1 1/3 cups.)
2. Chop the garlic and dill in a food processor. Add spinach, feta, zest, salt, and pepper. Whirl until cheese is finely grated, scraping down side of bowl as needed. Add drained yogurt. Pulse with on/off motion just until mixture is combined. Scrape into serving bowl. (Can be prepared a day ahead and refrigerated.)
Yield: Makes 2 cups.

ROASTED RED-PEPPER DIP

- 1 red onion, unpeeled, halved
- 2 pounds sweet red peppers
- 3 large cloves garlic, unpeeled
- 1/4 cup walnuts
- 3 tablespoons grated Parmesan cheese
- 2 teaspoons red-wine vinegar
- 3/4 teaspoon salt

1. Heat oven to 500°. Place onion and peppers on foil-lined pan.
2. Roast in 500° oven 20 minutes until darkened and wrinkled. Halfway through, add garlic and turn peppers.
3. Remove vegetables from oven. Wrap onion, peppers, and garlic in foil, crimping to seal. Let stand for 10 minutes.
4. Peel and seed peppers. Peel onion and garlic. Place vegetables, walnuts, cheese, vinegar, and salt in processor or blender. Whirl until smooth. Transfer to serving dish; chill. (Can be made 3 days ahead and refrigerated, covered.)
Yield: Makes 2 1/4 cups.

CAVIAR CREAM PUFFS

- 1 cup water
- 1/2 cup (1 stick) butter, cut in tablespoon pieces
- 1 cup all-purpose flour
- 5 eggs

Filling:

- 1/3 cup chopped fresh dill
- 1 container (16 ounces) reduced-fat sour cream
- 2 teaspoons grated lemon zest
- 4 ounces salmon or golden caviar
- Dill sprigs, for garnish

1. Prepare Puffs: Place both oven racks in middle positions in oven. Heat oven to 400°. Cover 2 large baking sheets with foil or parchment.
2. Bring water and butter to boiling in saucepan over high heat. As soon as mixture comes to boiling, add flour, stirring vigorously with wooden spoon; beat until dough pulls away from sides of pan, about 45 seconds. Remove from heat; cool 2 minutes, stirring constantly.
3. Beat in eggs, one at a time, beating after each until smooth and glossy.
4. Using rounded teaspoonfuls, spoon dough, about 1 inch apart, onto prepared baking sheets.
5. Bake in 400° oven on the 2 oven racks for 20 minutes or until puffed and golden, rotating pans from top to bottom halfway through baking.
6. Remove baking sheets from oven. Using a wooden pick or skewer, pierce a hole in bottom of each puff.
7. Turn oven off; return puffs to oven for 15 minutes or until dry and crisp. Remove the puffs to wire racks to cool completely.
8. Prepare Filling: Combine dill, sour cream, and zest in medium-size bowl.
9. Slice top off of each puff and reserve tops. Scoop out any excess dough from center of each puff with small spoon or fingers. Fill each puff with 1 slightly rounded teaspoonful of sour cream mixture. Top with heaping 1/4 teaspoon caviar. Place cream puff cap in place. Garnish with dab of sour cream mixture, dill, and remaining caviar.
Yield: Makes 5 dozen.

TEA-FLAVORED SHRIMP

4 **cups water**
1 **small onion, chopped (1/4 cup)**
1 **celery rib, chopped**
2 **jasmine-flavored tea bags**
Juice of 1 lemon (save lemon)
1 1/2 **pounds medium-size shrimp, shelled and deveined**

Hoisin Dipping Sauce:
2/3 **cup reduced-sodium chicken broth**
1/4 **cup reduced-sodium soy sauce**
3 **tablespoons hoisin sauce**
1 **tablespoon cornstarch**
1 **teaspoon dark sesame oil**
1/2 **teaspoon sugar**
1 **clove garlic, finely chopped**

1. Bring water to boiling in 5-quart Dutch oven over high heat. Add onion, celery, and tea bags. Reduce heat to medium; simmer 5 minutes. Remove tea bags. Add lemon juice and lemon; return to boiling.
2. Stir shrimp into the pot; cover and remove the pot from the heat. Let stand for 2 minutes or until the shrimp are pink and curled.
3. Meanwhile, prepare Hoisin Dipping Sauce: Whisk together chicken broth, soy sauce, hoisin sauce, cornstarch, sesame oil, sugar, and garlic in a small saucepan until cornstarch is completely dissolved and mixture is smooth. Bring to boiling over medium heat; cook, stirring occasionally, for 3 minutes or until the mixture is thickened slightly. Pour into small serving bowl.
4. Once the pot with the shrimp has stood for 2 minutes and the shrimp are cooked, drain them thoroughly. Serve with the sauce.
Yield: Makes 8 servings.

Succulent Tea-Flavored Shrimp (above) *are simmered in jasmine tea and served with a fragrant hoisin dipping sauce.* (Opposite, top) *Wrap a heady mix of mushrooms, wine, and seasonings in puff pastry for our crispy Mushroom Turnovers. A great example of what canned clams can become, Baked Clams are even more special if served in real clam shells (miniature pitas work well, too).*

MUSHROOM TURNOVERS

- 1 tablespoon butter or margarine
- 1 medium-size onion, chopped
- 1/4 pound button mushrooms, finely chopped
- 1/4 pound wild mushrooms, such as chanterelles or shitake, finely chopped
- 1 clove garlic, finely chopped
- 1 teaspoon salt
- 1/2 teaspoon dried leaf thyme
- 1/4 teaspoon ground black pepper
- 1/8 teaspoon dried rubbed sage
- 1/2 cup dry white wine
- 1 sheet frozen puff pastry (half of 17 1/4-ounce package), thawed according to package directions
- 1 egg, slightly beaten

1. Melt butter in large skillet over medium heat. Add onion; cook 2 minutes or until softened. Add mushrooms and garlic; sauté 3 minutes until mushrooms release liquid. Add salt, thyme, pepper, and sage; sauté 1 minute. Add wine; simmer 15 to 20 minutes or until all liquid has been absorbed. Cool.
2. Heat oven to 400°.
3. Meanwhile, roll out pastry on lightly floured surface to a 12 1/2-inch square. Neatly trim to 12-inch square. Cut sheet into sixteen 3-inch squares. Brush each square with a little egg. Spoon 1 slightly rounded tablespoon filling in center of each square. Fold each square of pastry in half diagonally into a triangle, bringing one corner to opposite corner. Gently pinch edges together to seal, making sure all the filling is sealed inside. With tines of fork, press edges together to seal. Cut a few small slashes in top of each turnover. Brush each turnover with some of the egg.
4. Bake in 400° oven for 15 minutes or until puffed and golden.
Make-Ahead Tip: If you wish, before baking, turnovers may be refrigerated several hours or frozen up to 2 weeks. Thaw before baking.
Yield: Makes 16 turnovers.

BAKED CLAMS

If you can get good-quality fresh clams from a reliable source, use them instead of the canned.

- 24 clam shell halves (about 2 inches) (see Note)
- 2 cans (6.5 ounces each) minced clams, undrained
- 1 teaspoon finely chopped garlic
- 2/3 cup seasoned sodium-free bread crumbs
- 1 ounce diced turkey pepperoni (about 1/4 cup)
- Lemon wedges, for garnish

1. Heat oven to 350°. Place clam shells on baking sheet.
2. Combine 2 cans undrained clams, garlic, and bread crumbs in small bowl. Spoon about 1 tablespoon clam mixture into each clam shell. Sprinkle with pepperoni.
3. Bake in 350° oven until heated through, about 10 minutes. Garnish with lemon wedges.
Note: Instead of clam shells, split 12 mini pita breads in half. Place on baking sheet; coat pitas with nonstick vegetable-oil cooking spray. Bake in 350° oven until crisp, about 10 minutes. Place about 1 tablespoon clam mixture on each and bake as above.
Yield: Makes 12 servings.

home sweet homes

CAPTURE THE ENCHANTMENT OF THE YULE SEASON WITH THESE WONDROUS COOKIE CREATIONS. ALL YOU "KNEAD" ARE TWO BASIC DOUGHS!

Who could resist nibbling at this star-struck Gingerbread Birdhouse? It's simple to assemble with royal icing for "mortar"; then you fancy it up with eye-catching confections. Candy wafers shingle a roof edged in icing, and a peppermint stick serves as a perch.

GINGERBREAD DOUGH

- 3 cups all-purpose flour
- 1 teaspoon baking soda
- 1/2 teaspoon salt
- 2 teaspoons ground ginger
- 1 teaspoon ground cinnamon
- 1/2 teaspoon grated nutmeg
- 1/4 teaspoon ground cloves
- 3/4 cup firmly packed dark-brown sugar
- 3/4 cup (1 1/2 sticks) unsalted butter, cut into pieces
- 1/4 cup unsulfured molasses
- 1/4 cup honey
- 1 egg

1. In medium bowl, sift together flour, baking soda, salt, ginger, cinnamon, nutmeg, and cloves until blended.
2. In food processor, combine brown sugar and butter. Whirl until mixture is smooth and creamy, about 1 minute. Add molasses, honey, and egg. Whirl until blended. Add flour mixture. Pulse with on/off motion just until dough clumps together.
3. Scrape dough onto sheet of plastic wrap; press together to form flat disk. Wrap; chill for 2 hours or overnight.
4. Heat oven to 350°. Lightly grease baking sheets.
5. Roll out dough onto floured surface to 1/8-inch thickness. Cut out cookies using desired cookie cutters. Place 1/2 inch apart on prepared baking sheets.
6. Bake in 350° oven for 12 to 14 minutes or until cookie edges begin to darken. Cool on baking sheets for a few minutes; transfer cookies to wire racks to cool completely.

ROYAL ICING

- 3 tablespoons meringue powder
- 4 cups confectioners' sugar
- 6 tablespoons warm water

1. In medium bowl, combine meringue powder, confectioners' sugar, and water.
2. Beat with an electric mixer 7 to 10 minutes or until icing is stiff.
Yield: Makes 3 cups.

GINGERBREAD BIRDHOUSE

- 1 recipe Gingerbread Dough (recipe, this page), with 1 teaspoon red paste food coloring added to molasses
- 2 recipes Royal Icing (recipe, this page)
- Paste food colors in red, black, yellow, and green
- Green leaf sugar sequins for wreath
- Small round red sugar sequins for wreath
- Silver dragées (see Note)
- Tiny red jawbreakers
- Small red disk candies
- Red fruit leather
- Thin candy wafers for shingles
- Candy stick for perch
- 2 to 3 square candies for presents
- 3 eight-inch pieces fine-gauge wire

You need: 8 x 9 x 1/2-inch foamcore board; paper to cover the board; tape; nonstick baking parchment.
Baking: Cover foamcore board with paper and secure with tape. Set aside. Heat oven to 350°. Cut baking parchment to match size of your baking sheets. Roll dough to 1/8-inch thickness. Cut following pieces according to patterns (pages 155-156): 1 front with holes, 1 back without holes, 2 sides, 2 roofs, 1 bird body, and 1 bird wing. Place on parchment. Score vertical lines into wall pieces about 1/2 inch apart. Add some dots of black paste food coloring to a small ball of dough and knead it in to marble dough, then roll and cut out the following pieces: 1 chimney front, 1 chimney back, 2 chimney sides, and 1 chimney top. Place on parchment. Score brick lines into chimney pieces. Bake in 350° oven for 12 to 14 minutes or until edges begin to darken. Cool on baking sheets for a few minutes; transfer to wire racks to cool completely.
Finishing: When the pieces are cool, make up 2 recipes Royal Icing. Color 1/2 cup of icing yellow. Fit a pastry bag with a coupler and #2 tip. Fill bag with yellow icing. (If you are a beginner at handling a pastry bag, you may want to

close the top with a rubber band to keep the icing inside.) Pipe yellow stars, swirls, and dots onto birdhouse walls while they are lying flat. Curl 1 end of each wire. Trace 3 stars (page, 155) onto a piece of nonstick baking parchment. Lay each wire flat on parchment so curled end is inside a star. Pipe yellow icing over wire to fill in star. Let dry. Fit a pastry bag with a coupler and #2 tip; fill with white icing. Pipe wreath around large hole on front wall, adding green and red sugar sequins as you go. Do about 1 inch at a time or icing will form a crust before you can finish. Pipe ribbons and bows on square candies to resemble presents. Let dry. Refer to photo (page 76) to frost and assemble bird. Let dry.

Assembling: To assemble walls on paper-covered board, lay walls facedown (as if they had been standing and then fallen straight out). Use a #6 tip to pipe a line of white icing on board where lower wall edges will attach. Pipe a line of icing at edges of back side of front wall where side walls will attach. Stand front and side walls up on board, fixing them to board and to each other at the same time. Pipe icing onto back side edges of back wall; fix to board and side walls. Allow icing to partially set. Pipe a wide line of icing to all wall upper edges. Place roof pieces, making sure overhangs are even at front and back. Hold in place about 2 minutes to give them a chance to set. Pipe a line of icing across the length of the roof peak. Rub white icing into the scored lines of the chimney pieces and wipe away any excess icing with a dry paper towel, leaving icing embedded in scored lines to look like mortar. Use icing to attach all chimney pieces to roof's center. Add chimney top last. Let dry.

Finishing: To shingle roof, use a #4 tip to pipe a line of white icing 1/4 inch from roof's bottom edge. Attach candy wafer shingles to icing in a straight line to make first row. For second row, pipe a line of icing 1/4 inch above first row. Cut or break one wafer in half vertically and begin row with this shingle. Continue row with whole wafers. This will offset shingle edges. Repeat icing and shingle steps, alternating rows, until whole roof is covered. You can add loops to roof edges, if desired. To make loops, use a #2 tip. Begin at one edge of roof, squeeze pastry bag to attach icing to roof edge. Continue squeezing and pulling downward 1/2 inch before reattaching 1/2 inch away. Always keep icing tip very clean and free of icing for this process since icing tends to stick to itself on the tip. Top roof with a row of small red disk candies and top each of those with a tiny red jawbreaker. Cut a 4-inch length of candy stick and insert it into perch hole. Pipe some icing around candy stick to anchor perch. Use a #18 (star) tip to pipe beads on all seams, roof edges, and around house's base. Add a row of tiny red jawbreakers to the front roof edge with icing. When icing stars are dry, insert other wire ends into bird; affix bird to chimney top with icing. Attach presents to perch and fruit leather bow to wreath with icing. Let dry.

Note: Silver dragées are not recognized by the Food and Drug Administration as edible. Use for decoration only; remove before eating cookie.

STAINED-GLASS COOKIE HOUSES

1 1/2 cups all-purpose flour
2 teaspoons ground ginger
1 teaspoon ground cinnamon
1/2 teaspoon ground nutmeg
1/4 teaspoon ground cloves
1/4 cup dark molasses
24 ounces refrigerated sugar-cookie dough
6 rolls hard, clear candies
Royal Icing (recipe, page 77)
Paste food coloring OR soft gel food colors

1. Heat oven to 350°.
2. Combine flour, ginger, cinnamon, nutmeg, and cloves in large bowl. Add molasses and beat on low speed to blend. Break dough into pieces and add to flour mixture. Beat on low speed until ingredients are blended together but mixture is still crumbly. Transfer to work surface; knead until dough comes together. Divide into fourths. Shape each fourth into disk; wrap in plastic wrap and refrigerate 30 minutes.
3. Roll out 1 disk on lightly floured sheet of foil to a scant 1/4-inch thickness. Cut 8 x 6-inch rectangle from dough; reserve scraps to reroll. Trim rectangle to desired house shape, leaving it on foil. Use paring knife to cut out and remove dough for windows and door. Use a drinking straw to make holes for hanging. Carefully transfer dough on foil to baking sheet.
4. Bake in 350° oven 10 to 12 minutes or until cookie is baked through and firm. Transfer cookie on foil to wire rack to cool.
5. Separate like-colored candies into different resealable plastic bags; lightly break up candies with meat mallet or hammer. Spoon broken candies into window and door openings on cookie to just fill. (Mix colors for a stained-glass look.)
6. Return cookie to oven. Bake in 350° oven until candies have melted, 3 to 4 minutes. Transfer cookie on foil to wire rack to cool completely. Carefully remove foil from back of cookie.
7. Repeat with remaining cookie dough, including scraps, and candies.
8. Tint Royal Icing to desired colors. Spoon icing into a pastry bag fitted with #2 round pastry tip. Pipe designs onto cookies. Let icing dry until set, about 45 minutes.
Yield: Makes 6 large cookies.

From making to baking, scrumptious Stained-Glass Cookie Houses take only minutes. The secret? Store-bought sugar-cookie dough. Roll it out, cut the cottages, then crumble hard candies in windows. The bright candy bits will melt into panes in the oven. Frost elaborately, of course.

SCHOOL
BANK
36

Glazed Gingerbread Coffee Cake (opposite) *can be made in advance and warmed up in a flash, as can homey Black Forest Bread Pudding* (above, left). *Maple syrup adds flavor to our mulled Maple Cider Toddy* (not shown), *and Fruit Compote* (right) *is spiced with cinnamon.*

MAPLE CIDER TODDY

4 cups apple cider
3 tablespoons maple syrup
½ vanilla bean, split
1 cinnamon stick
12 whole allspice berries
1 cup brandy OR applejack
Cinnamon sticks, for garnish (optional)

1. Combine cider, maple syrup, vanilla, cinnamon, and allspice in nonaluminum saucepan. Simmer, covered, for 25 minutes. Strain; discard solids. Return liquid to saucepan.
2. To serve: Stir in brandy. Garnish with cinnamon sticks, if desired.
Yield: Makes 8 drinks.

BLACK FOREST BREAD PUDDING

6 cups Italian bread cubes
¾ cup dried cherries
2½ cups low-fat milk
½ cup granulated sugar
8 ounces semisweet chocolate, chopped
3 eggs
1 egg white
⅓ cup confectioners' sugar
Whipped cream (optional)

1. Mix bread and cherries in bowl. Bring milk and granulated sugar in saucepan to boiling. Stir in chocolate until almost melted. Remove from heat; stir until smooth. Cool to room temperature.
2. Whisk eggs and white in small bowl. Add to chocolate mixture. Pour over bread. Cover; let stand 30 minutes.
3. Heat oven to 325°. Butter 11 x 7 x 2-inch baking pan. Pour bread mixture into pan. Cover tightly with buttered aluminum foil.
4. Bake in 325° oven for 30 minutes. Remove foil; cool slightly. Dust with confectioners' sugar and serve with whipped cream, if you wish.
Yield: Makes 8 servings.

FRUIT COMPOTE

Accent each Fruit Compote with a dollop of yogurt and sprinkle with lemon zest.

1 cup water
Juice (about ¼ cup) and grated zest of 1 lemon
¼ cup sugar
1 cup dried apricots (about 6 ounces)
1 cup pitted prunes with lemon essence (about 6 ounces)
½ cup golden raisins
½ cup dried cherries OR dried cranberries
1 navel orange
1 cinnamon stick
2 tablespoons orange-flavored liqueur
1 quart nonfat vanilla yogurt

1. Combine water, lemon juice, and sugar in saucepan. Add apricots, prunes, raisins, and cherries.
2. Cut orange in half lengthwise, then slice crosswise into semicircles. Cut semicircles in half. Gently stir into dried fruit mixture in saucepan. Add lemon zest and cinnamon stick. Cover; simmer for 10 minutes. Add liqueur; simmer, uncovered, for 5 minutes.
3. Serve warm or cold with yogurt.
Yield: Makes 12 servings.

bright & early brunch

IT'S CHRISTMAS MORNING...THE GIFTS HAVE BEEN OPENED, THE STOCKINGS UNSTUFFED...AND EVERYONE'S READY TO EAT! FOLLOW OUR LEAD TO SERVE UP AN EXTRA-SPECIAL BRUNCH. PREP THE NIGHT BEFORE SO YOU CAN ENJOY THE FUN.

BAKED FRENCH TOAST WITH 3 SAUCES

- **3 tablespoons melted butter**
- **1 1/2 cups milk**
- **3 eggs**
- **2 tablespoons confectioners' sugar**
- **1 teaspoon vanilla**
- **1/2 teaspoon ground cinnamon**
- **1/8 teaspoon ground nutmeg**
- **6 slices egg bread (challah), cut into 1-inch-thick slices**
- **Caramel-Apple Cream**
- **No-Cook Strawberry Sauce**
- **Maple-Walnut Butter**

1. Heat oven to 475°.
2. Drizzle melted butter onto a 17 x 11-inch jelly-roll pan.
3. Whisk together milk, eggs, confectioners' sugar, vanilla, cinnamon, and nutmeg in large bowl. Dip both sides of bread into milk mixture; place on prepared pan. Pour any remaining milk mixture over bread. Let stand 20 minutes, turning bread over a couple of times.
4. Bake in 475° oven, turning once, until puffed and golden, for about 15 minutes. Serve with 3 sauces.
Yield: Makes 6 servings.

NO-COOK STRAWBERRY SAUCE

- **1 pint strawberries, washed and hulled**
- **3 tablespoons sugar**
- **2 tablespoons orange liqueur OR orange juice**
- **Fresh mint sprigs, for garnish (optional)**

1. Coarsely chop 1/2 cup of the strawberries. Quarter remaining strawberries lengthwise.
2. Combine strawberries, sugar, and orange liqueur or juice in a bowl. Let stand 15 minutes or until sugar is completely melted. Serve with French toast. Garnish with mint, if desired.
Yield: Makes 1 1/2 cups.

MAPLE-WALNUT BUTTER

- **1/2 cup (1 stick) butter, at room temperature**
- **1/2 cup finely chopped walnuts**
- **1/4 cup maple syrup OR pancake syrup**

Stir together butter, walnuts, and syrup in small bowl until well blended. Refrigerate until ready to use. To soften, remove from refrigerator 15 minutes before using. Serve with French toast.
Yield: Makes 1 1/4 cups.

CARAMEL-APPLE CREAM

- **1/4 cup (1/2 stick) butter**
- **2 medium-size Golden Delicious apples, peeled, cored, and thinly sliced**
- **1/4 cup firmly packed light-brown sugar**
- **3 tablespoons half-and-half**
- **1/8 teaspoon ground allspice**
- **Confectioners' sugar, for dusting (optional)**

Heat the butter in a 12-inch skillet over medium heat. Add the apple slices; cook until the slices are softened slightly, about 5 minutes. Add the brown sugar, half-and-half, and allspice, stirring occasionally, until the mixture is melted, smooth, and thickened slightly, about 2 minutes. Spoon the sauce over each serving of French toast. Dust with confectioners' sugar, if desired.
Yield: Makes 1 1/2 cups.

Feed one and all with easy-on-you Baked French Toast. You make the three sauces and eggy mix in advance, then simply dip the bread slices and slide 'em in the oven. Serve luscious strawberry, maple-walnut, and caramel-apple sauces in pretty bowls.

GINGERBREAD COFFEE CAKE

- 1 cup water
- 1 cup molasses
- 1 teaspoon baking soda
- 1 cup firmly packed brown sugar
- 1/2 cup (1 stick) butter, softened
- 2 eggs, beaten
- 2 cups all-purpose flour
- 1 tablespoon baking powder
- 1 teaspoon ground cinnamon
- 1/4 teaspoon ground ginger
- 1/4 teaspoon ground cloves

Topping:
- 1/3 cup all-purpose flour
- 1/3 cup granulated sugar
- 1/4 teaspoon ground cinnamon
- 1/4 teaspoon ground ginger
- 1/2 cup chopped walnuts
- 3 tablespoons butter

Glaze:
- 1 cup confectioners' sugar
- 1 1/2 tablespoons milk
- 1/2 teaspoon vanilla

1. Heat oven to 350°. Grease 13 x 9 x 2-inch baking pan. Bring water and molasses in saucepan to boiling. Stir in baking soda. Let cool.
2. Beat brown sugar, butter, and eggs in bowl. In second bowl, combine flour, baking powder, cinnamon, ginger, and cloves. Beat flour mixture alternately with molasses, half at a time, into butter mixture until well mixed. Pour into the prepared pan.
3. Prepare Topping: Combine flour, granulated sugar, cinnamon, ginger, and walnuts in small bowl. Cut in butter with pastry blender until mixture is coarsely crumbled. Sprinkle over gingerbread.
4. Bake in 350° oven for 40 minutes or until wooden pick inserted in center comes out clean.
5. Prepare Glaze: Whisk confectioners' sugar, milk, and vanilla in small bowl until soft enough to drip from spoon. If needed, add more milk for proper consistency. Drizzle over top of cake.
Yield: Makes 12 servings.

GLACÉ FRUIT-FILLED COFFEE CAKE

- 1 cup chopped glacé fruits
- 3/4 cup chopped walnuts
- 2 teaspoons grated lemon zest
- 1 tablespoon honey
- 3 1/2 cups all-purpose flour
- 1/3 cup plus 1/4 cup sugar
- 1/2 teaspoon salt
- 1 envelope quick-rise yeast
- 3/4 cup plain yogurt
- 1/4 cup water
- 6 tablespoons butter or margarine
- 1 egg
- 2 teaspoons lemon juice
- 1/2 teaspoon ground cinnamon
- White Glaze (recipe follows)
- Glacé fruits (optional)

1. Combine glacé fruits, 1/2 cup of the walnuts, 1 teaspoon of the grated lemon zest, and honey in small bowl.
2. Combine 2 cups flour, 1/3 cup sugar, salt, and yeast in large bowl.
3. Combine yogurt, water, and 4 tablespoons of the butter in small saucepan. Heat to 130° (mixture will be comfortably hot to the touch). Add to flour mixture. Add egg, lemon juice, and remaining lemon zest. Blend with electric mixer at slow speed, then beat at medium speed for 3 minutes. Gradually stir in 1 cup of remaining flour to make a soft dough.
4. Turn dough out onto lightly floured surface. Knead until smooth and elastic, 5 to 10 minutes, adding more flour as needed to prevent sticking. Place dough in large oiled bowl, turning to coat. Cover with a towel. Let rise in warm place, away from drafts, until doubled, for about 30 minutes.
5. Punch dough down. Let rest for 10 minutes.
6. Combine remaining 1/4 cup sugar, the remaining 1/4 cup of walnuts, and the cinnamon in small bowl.
7. Melt remaining 2 tablespoons of butter in small saucepan or microwave oven. Brush half of butter over bottom and sides of 12-cup Bundt pan. Sprinkle bottom of pan with half of cinnamon-sugar mixture.
8. Roll dough out onto lightly floured surface into 15 x 9-inch rectangle. Cut into fifteen 3-inch squares. Spoon 1 tablespoon of fruit-nut mixture into center of each square. Bring opposite corners together; pinch to seal, making a square.
9. Stand squares on edge, side by side, spoke-fashion, in prepared pan. Brush with remaining butter. Sprinkle with remaining cinnamon-sugar mixture. Cover and let rise in warm place, away from drafts, until doubled, 30 to 35 minutes.
10. Heat oven to 375°.
11. Bake in 375° oven for 30 minutes or until browned. Invert onto wire rack to cool.
12. Pour White Glaze over coffee cake. Decorate with glacé fruits, if desired.
White Glaze: Place 1 cup sifted confectioners' sugar in small bowl. Gradually stir in 1 to 2 tablespoons milk until glaze is smooth and pourable.
Yield: Makes 16 servings.

CRUSTY POTATO BAKE

- 1 pound small red potatoes, cut into eighths
- 2 medium-size onions, cut into 1-inch pieces
- 1 sweet red pepper, cut into 1-inch pieces
- 2 cloves garlic, finely chopped
- 1 tablespoon olive oil
- 1 tablespoon butter
- 1 teaspoon chopped fresh rosemary OR 1/4 teaspoon dried rosemary
- 1/2 teaspoon salt
- 1/2 teaspoon ground black pepper
- 1 can (8 ounces) artichoke hearts, drained and quartered
- 4 ounces Canadian bacon, diced
- 1 container (8 ounces) nonfat sour cream
- 4 ounces reduced-fat cream cheese, at room temperature
- 1 1/2 cups plus 1/2 cup shredded Cheddar cheese (8 ounces)
- 1/3 cup flavored bread crumbs
- 1 tablespoon chopped parsley

1. Heat oven to 375°. Combine potatoes, onions, red pepper, garlic, olive oil, butter, rosemary, salt, and black pepper in a large bowl. Spoon into 9 x 9 x 2-inch-square flameproof baking dish.
2. Bake in 375° oven, stirring occasionally, 45 minutes or until potatoes are almost cooked. Remove from oven. Add artichokes and bacon to potatoes. (Recipe can be prepared ahead up to this point.)
3. Beat sour cream and cream cheese until creamy. Stir in the 1 1/2 cups Cheddar. Spread over casserole.
4. Bake in 375° oven 15 minutes. Remove from oven. Increase oven temperature to broil. Mix crumbs, remaining 1/2 cup Cheddar, and parsley. Sprinkle over casserole. Broil until golden brown, 1 minute.
Yield: Makes 6 servings.

What a show-stopper! Glacé Fruit-Filled Coffee Cake will have guests coming back for seconds. For a hearty, savory main dish, serve up Crusty Potato Bake (not shown).

Stir added flavor into Frothy Mexi-Mocha Coffee (above) with a fragrant cinnamon stick. The deep-dish Torta Rustica (opposite) is filled with Italian turkey sausage, provolone, ricotta, and other tastes. It's even better when you make it a few days beforehand and reheat.

FROTHY MEXI-MOCHA COFFEE

- **½ cup firmly packed light-brown sugar**
- **6 ounces semisweet chocolate, chopped**
- **1 large strip orange zest**
- **¼ teaspoon ground allspice**
- **½ teaspoon ground cinnamon**
- **4½ cups hot strong coffee**
- **¾ cup half-and-half, warmed**
- **Orange zest, cinnamon sticks, chocolate-covered coffee beans, for garnish (optional)**

Whirl brown sugar, chocolate, zest, allspice, and cinnamon in blender to chop finely. Add coffee. Whirl until chocolate is melted and mixture is smooth. Add warmed half-and half. Whirl until frothy. Strain. Serve in cups. Garnish with zest, cinnamon sticks, and coffee beans, if you wish.
Yield: Makes 6 cups.

TORTA RUSTICA

- **2 teaspoons olive oil**
- **1 onion, chopped**
- **2 cloves garlic, chopped**
- **½ pound Italian turkey sausage links, sliced**
- **1 container (32 ounces) part-skim-milk ricotta cheese**
- **3 eggs, beaten**
- **½ pound sliced provolone cheese, cut into strips**
- **¼ pound prosciutto, diced**
- **⅓ cup grated Parmesan cheese**
- **¼ teaspoon salt**
- **¼ teaspoon ground black pepper**
- **1 package refrigerated ready-to-use piecrust (2 crusts)**
- **1 egg yolk, beaten**

1. Heat oven to 375°. Coat 10-inch springform pan with nonstick vegetable-oil cooking spray.
2. Heat oil in medium-size nonstick skillet over medium heat. Add onion and garlic; sauté for 5 minutes. Add sausage slices; sauté until cooked through, about 10 minutes. Remove skillet from the heat.
3. Combine ricotta, eggs, provolone, prosciutto, Parmesan, salt, and pepper in large bowl. Stir in the sausage mixture.
4. Roll out both piecrusts on lightly floured surface with lightly floured rolling pin to two 14-inch rounds. Place one round in bottom of prepared pan. With fingers, lightly press crust into bottom and up sides of pan, without stretching dough.
5. Spoon cheese mixture into pastry-lined pan. Place second crust on top of cheese mixture; trim edges of pastry even with rim of pan. Brush pastry with beaten egg yolk.
6. Bake on the bottom oven rack in 375° oven for 45 minutes. (If the top begins to brown too quickly, cover with sheet of aluminum foil.) Turn oven off; let the pie continue to cook in the oven for another 15 minutes or until a knife inserted in the center comes out clean.
Yield: Makes 12 servings.

glorious goodies

EVERYONE LOVES HOLIDAY SWEETS, SO WHIP UP A BATCH OF THESE GLORIOUS GOODIES AND WATCH THEM GO FAST! THEY'RE SIMPLY DELICIOUS, AND A SNAP TO MAKE.

Don't be surprised if these bite-size treats disappear in a wink! A splash of cream makes Chocolate-Pecan Thumbprints (top row, from left) *especially rich. Sprinkles add a festive look to Choco-Cherry Truffles. Cranberry Roll-Ups begin with frozen puff pastry. Mint Meltaways* (second row, from center) *are luscious brownies with peppermint frosting, and Maple-Walnut Cakes feature sweet potato batter. Layer two different doughs and slice to create Ginger Checkerboards* (third row, center).

CHOCOLATE-PECAN THUMBPRINTS

- 2 cups all-purpose flour
- 1 cup finely ground pecans
- 1/4 teaspoon salt
- 3/4 cup (1 1/2 sticks) unsalted butter, at room temperature
- 1/2 cup granulated sugar
- 1/2 cup confectioners' sugar
- 2 eggs
- 2 teaspoons vanilla
- 1/3 cup heavy cream
- 4 squares (1 ounce each) semisweet chocolate, finely chopped
- 4 1/2 dozen pecan halves (optional)

1. Heat oven to 350°.
2. Mix together flour, pecans, and salt in medium-size bowl.
3. Beat together butter and sugars in second medium-size bowl until light and fluffy, about 3 minutes. Beat in eggs, one at a time, until well blended. Beat in vanilla. On low speed, beat in flour mixture just until dough forms. Cover and refrigerate for at least 1 hour for dough to firm up.
4. Using 2 teaspoons dough for each thumbprint, roll dough between palms into balls. Transfer to ungreased baking sheet, spacing 1 1/2 inches apart. With wooden spoon handle or finger, make slight indentation in top of each cookie.
5. Bake in 350° oven for 10 to 11 minutes or until lightly browned. Let cookies cool slightly on baking sheets on wire racks. Then transfer the cookies to wire racks to cool completely.
6. Meanwhile, while cookies are cooling, heat cream in small saucepan just until small bubbles appear around edge. Pour over chocolate in small bowl, stirring to melt the chocolate completely. Let cool slightly.
7. Spoon slightly cooled chocolate into the indentations in the cookies. If using the pecans, press a pecan half into the chocolate on each cookie. Then let stand at room temperature until the chocolate sets, or refrigerate the cookies for a quick set.
Yield: Makes about 4 1/2 dozen cookies.

CRANBERRY ROLL-UPS

- 1 cup cranberries
- 1/3 cup firmly packed light-brown sugar
- 1/8 teaspoon ground cinnamon
- Pinch ground nutmeg
- 1/2 cup dried apricots
- 2 tablespoons apple or cranberry juice
- 1 package (17.3 ounces) frozen puff pastry sheets, thawed according to package directions
- 1/2 cup walnuts, coarsely chopped

1. Combine cranberries, brown sugar, cinnamon, nutmeg, apricots, and juice in small saucepan. Bring to boiling over medium-high heat. Cover; reduce heat to medium-low. Cook for 8 minutes or until thickened.
2. Transfer cranberry mixture to food processor or blender. Purée until almost completely smooth, but still with some small pieces; you should have about 1 cup filling. Set filling aside to cool.
3. Heat oven to 425°.
4. Unroll 1 pastry sheet on flat surface. Spread half the cranberry filling over pastry. Cut sheet in half lengthwise; cut each half crosswise into 8 equal strips. Roll up each strip, enclosing filling. Repeat with remaining sheet of pastry and filling, to make a total of 32 roll-ups.
5. Spoon about 1/2 teaspoon chopped nuts into each of 32 cups (1 3/4 x 3/4 inch) in mini-muffin pans (3 pans). Place a roll-up, cut side up, in each cup.
6. Bake one pan in 425° oven for 15 to 18 minutes or until roll-ups are puffed and golden. Transfer roll-ups to rack to cool. (While baking one mini-muffin pan, keep other pans refrigerated. Or, if you have only one mini-muffin pan, refrigerate other unbaked roll-ups. After baking one batch, let pan cool. Then wash and dry the pan and proceed with the other batches of roll-ups.)
7. Serve roll-ups slightly warm or at room temperature.
Yield: Makes about 2 3/4 dozen.

CHOCO-CHERRY TRUFFLES

- 12 squares (1 ounce each) semisweet chocolate
- 3 squares (1 ounce each) unsweetened chocolate
- 1 can (about 14 ounces) sweetened condensed milk
- 1/4 teaspoon salt
- 2 tablespoons cherry-flavored liqueur (optional)
- 1/4 cup chopped nuts
- 1/2 cup maraschino cherries, drained and chopped
- 2 packages (6 ounces each) premium white chocolate baking bars
- 2 teaspoons vegetable oil
- Assorted colored sprinkles

1. Heat semisweet and unsweetened chocolate, sweetened condensed milk, and salt in saucepan over medium heat, stirring, until chocolate is melted, about 7 minutes. Remove from heat. Add liqueur, if using, and nuts and cherries. Cover surface directly with waxed paper; refrigerate until cold, 1 1/2 hours.
2. Shape slightly heaping tablespoonfuls of chocolate mixture into smooth balls. Place on waxed paper-lined baking sheet.
3. Melt white chocolate with oil in small saucepan over low heat, stirring. Let stand until cool to touch, 1 minute. Using 2 forks, dip balls into white chocolate. Transfer to waxed paper to dry. Decorate with sprinkles.
Yield: Makes 3 1/2 dozen candies.

MAPLE-WALNUT CAKES

Cakes:

- 2 cups all-purpose flour
- 1 tablespoon baking powder
- 1 teaspoon baking soda
- 1 teaspoon ground cinnamon
- 1/2 cup (1 stick) unsalted butter, at room temperature
- 3/4 cup granulated sugar
- 1/2 cup maple syrup
- 2 eggs
- 1 can (about 16 ounces) sweet potatoes in syrup
- 1/2 teaspoon maple extract
- 3/4 cup walnuts, chopped

Frosting:

- 1/4 cup heavy cream
- 12 ounces cream cheese, softened
- 1/4 teaspoon maple extract
- 6 tablespoons (3/4 stick) unsalted butter, at room temperature
- 1 pound confectioners' sugar
- Red and green glacé cherries, for garnish

1. Heat oven to 350°. Grease and flour three 8 x 2-inch round cake pans.
2. Prepare Cakes: Sift flour, baking powder, baking soda, and cinnamon into bowl.
3. Beat butter in second bowl until smooth and creamy. Beat in granulated sugar and maple syrup. Add eggs, one at a time, beating after each addition. Drain potatoes; purée in food processor or mash with fork. Add potatoes and maple extract to butter mixture; beat until smooth. On low speed, beat in flour mixture just until incorporated. Fold in walnuts. Transfer batter to pans, dividing evenly.
4. Bake in 350° oven for 25 to 30 minutes or until golden brown. Cool in pans on rack 10 minutes. Remove cakes to rack to cool completely.
5. Prepare Frosting: Beat cream, cream cheese, maple extract, and butter in bowl until smooth. Add confectioners' sugar; beat until good spreading consistency. If necessary, refrigerate to thicken if butter becomes too soft.
6. Sandwich cake layers together with 3/4 cup frosting between each layer. Frost top and sides of cake. Garnish with glacé cherries.
Variation: For small snacking cakes, pour batter in greased, floured 15 x 10 x 1 1/2-inch jelly-roll pan. Bake in 350° oven for 20 to 25 minutes. Cool as layer cake. Frost and cut into small squares or diamonds. Garnish with cherries.
Yield: Makes 12 cake slices or 4 dozen squares.

GINGER CHECKERBOARDS

- 3/4 cup (1 1/2 sticks) unsalted butter, at room temperature
- 3/4 cup sugar
- 1 egg
- 1 1/2 teaspoons vanilla
- 1 tablespoon ground ginger
- 1/2 teaspoon ground white pepper
- 1/4 teaspoon salt
- 1/4 cup mild-flavored molasses
- 3 cups all-purpose flour
- 1/4 cup light corn syrup

1. Beat together butter and sugar in large bowl until creamy, about 3 minutes. Add egg and vanilla; beat well. Beat in ginger, pepper, and salt. Divide mixture in half and set half aside. Beat molasses into remaining half of butter mixture in bowl. On low speed, beat in 1 1/2 cups of the flour until a dough forms.
2. Transfer dough to sheet of plastic wrap; top with second piece of wrap. Roll into 10 x 8-inch rectangle, about 1/3 inch thick. Transfer to baking sheet; refrigerate 1 hour or until hardened.
3. Beat corn syrup into reserved half of butter mixture. On low speed, beat in remaining 1 1/2 cups flour until a dough forms.
4. Transfer light-colored dough to plastic wrap; top with second piece of wrap. Roll into 10 x 8-inch rectangle, about 1/3 inch thick. Transfer to baking sheet; refrigerate 1 hour or until hardened. Repeat with darker dough.
5. To assemble: Remove dough from refrigerator; discard plastic wrap. Using sharp knife, slice both doughs lengthwise into thin strips, about 1/3 inch wide.
6. Lay light-colored strip on work surface. Lay darker strip next to it, then another light strip next to it; gently press strips together. Top strips with second and third row, alternating colors, to make a block, 3 strips wide and 3 strips high; gently press together. Refrigerate or freeze until hardened. Repeat with remaining strips until all dough is used, alternating colors in base row: 2 dark strips and 1 light, 2 lights and 1 dark, etc. If dough tears, gently press together and freeze for 15 minutes to harden.
7. Heat oven to 375°. Remove blocks from refrigerator or freezer; slice crosswise into 1/4-inch-thick cookies. Transfer to ungreased baking sheets; reshape slightly if necessary.
8. Bake in 375° oven for 10 minutes or until the lighter portions are slightly golden. Let cool slightly on baking sheets on wire rack. Transfer cookies to wire racks to cool completely.
Yield: Makes 4 dozen cookies.

MINT MELTAWAYS

- 1 1/2 cups (3 sticks) butter
- 6 squares (1 ounce each) unsweetened chocolate
- 6 eggs
- 2 1/2 cups granulated sugar
- 2 teaspoons vanilla
- 1 1/2 cups all-purpose flour
- 1 1/4 teaspoons peppermint extract

Peppermint Frosting:

- 1 pound confectioners' sugar
- 6 tablespoons heavy cream
- 1/4 cup (1/2 stick) butter, at room temperature
- 1/4 teaspoon peppermint extract
- 1/4 cup crushed peppermints

1. Heat oven to 350°. Line 15 x 10 x 1 1/2-inch jelly-roll pan with waxed paper. Coat with nonstick vegetable-oil cooking spray.
2. Melt butter and chocolate in saucepan. Beat in eggs, granulated sugar, and vanilla. Stir in flour and peppermint extract. Spread batter in pan.
3. Bake in 350° oven for 30 minutes or until edges begin to firm. Remove pan to wire rack to cool.
4. Prepare Peppermint Frosting: Beat confectioners sugar, cream, butter, and peppermint extract in bowl until smooth. Lift brownie out of pan. Frost top. Sprinkle with candies. Cut into squares or mini-squares.
Yield: Makes 4 dozen bars.

ALMOND SHORTBREAD

- 1 1/4 cups all-purpose flour
- 1/3 cup unblanched almonds, finely chopped
- 1/4 teaspoon salt
- 1/2 cup (1 stick) butter, at room temperature
- 1/3 cup granulated sugar
- 1 teaspoon vanilla
- 1 teaspoon almond extract
- 1/2 cup semisweet chocolate chips, for drizzle
- Confectioners' sugar, for garnish

1. Heat oven to 350°. Lightly grease large baking sheet.
2. Stir together flour, almonds, and salt in a small bowl.
3. Beat together butter, granulated sugar, vanilla, and almond extract in medium-size bowl until creamy and smooth, about 2 minutes. Stir in flour mixture.
4. Divide the dough into 4 equal balls. On a greased baking sheet, pat or roll out each ball of dough to 4 1/2-inch round. Smooth edge. Press with tines of fork all around edge, if desired. Cut each round into 6 equal wedges, but do not pull the wedges apart.
5. Bake in 350° oven for 12 to 14 minutes or until lightly browned at edges. While still hot, recut the rounds into wedges and remove to a wire rack to cool completely.
6. Melt semisweet chocolate chips in small bowl in microwave oven or over pan of hot water. Drizzle over wedges. Sprinkle evenly with confectioners' sugar. Store shortbread in airtight container. You can redust shortbread with confectioners' sugar just before serving.
Yield: Makes 2 dozen cookies.

PECAN LOGS

Prepare Almond Shortbread dough, substituting 1/3 cup ground pecans for chopped almonds and omitting almond extract. Pinch off pieces of dough in rounded teaspoonfuls. Roll into logs, dip into water, and roll in 1/2 cup finely chopped pecans to coat. Bake in 350° oven for 12 to 14 minutes; cool on wire rack. Dip one end in melted semisweet chocolate.
Yield: Makes about 2 1/2 dozen logs.

CARAMEL BONBONS

Prepare Almond Shortbread dough, halving vanilla and almond extracts. Beat 1 egg yolk into butter-sugar mixture. Divide dough into 20 equal balls. Cut 5 small caramel candies into quarters. In palm of hand, flatten one ball of dough into 2-inch round. Press piece of caramel into center of dough and securely pinch closed. Reshape into ball and place on greased baking sheet. Repeat with remaining dough and caramel pieces, spacing bonbons 2 inches apart. Brush tops of balls with lightly beaten egg white; sprinkle with coarse decorating sugar crystals. Bake in 350° oven for 12 to 14 minutes or until lightly colored; be careful not to overbake or bonbons will split. Transfer bonbons to wire rack to cool. Store in airtight containers at room temperature.
Yield: Makes 20 bonbons.

So many alternatives mean you're going to have goodies galore — lots to keep and enjoy, plus plenty to give away. Our pleasingly nutty Almond Shortbread (top) *looks oh-so-very merry. For a fabulous finish, dip the end of each Pecan Log* (middle) *in melted chocolate. Every Caramel Bonbon* (bottom) *has a yummy piece of candy in the center.*

VANILLA COOKIES

A basic vanilla-flavored dough is the start for an assortment of holiday cookies. With simple additions and substitutions, you can make 7 scrumptious kinds.

1 1/4 cups all-purpose flour
1/2 teaspoon baking powder
1/4 teaspoon salt
3 tablespoons unsalted butter, at room temperature
3 tablespoons margarine, at room temperature
1/2 cup granulated sugar
1 egg
1/2 teaspoon vanilla
Vanilla Glaze (recipe follows)

1. Stir together flour, baking powder, and salt in medium-size bowl.
2. Beat butter, margarine, sugar, egg, and vanilla in bowl until well blended. Stir in flour mixture. Shape into ball; wrap in plastic wrap; refrigerate several hours or overnight.
3. Heat oven to 350°. Coat cookie sheet with nonstick vegetable-oil cooking spray.
4. Roll out dough on lightly floured surface to 3/8-inch thickness. Cut into rounds with 2 1/2-inch cookie cutter. Place on prepared cookie sheets, space 1 1/2 inches apart.
5. Bake in 350° oven for 10 to 12 minutes or until lightly browned at edges. Remove cookies to wire rack to cool. Frost with glaze, if you wish.
Yield: Makes 2 1/2 dozen cookies.

Vanilla Glaze

Gradually stir 1 to 2 tablespoons milk into 1 cup confectioners' sugar until smooth and slightly runny. Add 1/4 teaspoon vanilla.

Lemon or Lime Glaze
Omit vanilla and substitute lemon juice or lime juice for milk in Vanilla Glaze.

White Icing
Omit vanilla and use water rather than milk in Vanilla Glaze. Tint with food coloring, if desired.

COOKIE DOUGH VARIATIONS

Refer to Vanilla Cookie recipe.

Spice: Omit vanilla. Substitute 1/4 cup firmly packed dark-brown sugar for 1/4 cup of the granulated sugar. Stir 1 teaspoon ground ginger and 1/4 teaspoon each cinnamon and allspice into flour mixture.
Lime: Omit vanilla. Add 2 teaspoons each grated lime zest and lime juice to butter mixture.
Lemon: Omit vanilla. Add 1 1/2 teaspoons each grated lemon zest and lemon juice to butter mixture.
Mint: Omit vanilla. Add 1/4 teaspoon mint extract to butter mixture.
Chocolate: Add 2 tablespoons unsweetened cocoa powder to flour mixture.
Orange: Omit vanilla. Add 1 teaspoon grated orange zest to butter mixture.
Maple Walnut: Omit vanilla. Substitute 1/4 cup firmly packed light-brown sugar for 1/4 cup of the granulated sugar; add 1/2 cup finely chopped walnuts to flour mixture.
Almond: Omit vanilla. Add 1/2 teaspoon almond extract to butter mixture. Add 1/2 cup finely chopped toasted blanched almonds to flour mixture.

COOKIE SHAPES

Spice Kids: Cut chilled Spice Cookie dough into 16 pieces. Roll, cut out kids, bake as in Vanilla Cookies. Remove from pan to rack to cool. Pipe on outline and decorations with White Icing.
Lime Slices: Cut out rolled-out Lime Cookie dough with 2 1/4-inch round cookie cutter. Cut rounds in half. Place on cookie sheet. Bake as directed. When cool, frost with Lime Glaze. Divide into "segments" with White Icing and outline bottoms with dark green-tinted White Icing.
Lemon Blossoms: Place Lemon Cookie dough, chilled for 1 hour, in cookie gun with blossom tip. Press out onto cookie sheet following package directions. Bake as directed. When cool, frost with Lemon Glaze; sprinkle with chopped pistachio nuts.
Mint Candy Canes: Cut out rolled-out Mint Cookie dough with 4-inch candy cane cutter. Place on cookie sheet. Bake as directed. When cool, frost with Vanilla Glaze. Add red licorice stripes and sprinkle with chopped peppermint candies.
Choco-Orange Bull's Eyes: With half the Chocolate Cookie dough, make an equal number of cookie balls, using a rounded measuring teaspoon and a rounded measuring half teaspoon. Repeat with half the Orange Cookie dough. Press an indentation into large balls. Press small balls into indentations, using both doughs for each cookie. Place on cookie sheet. Bake as directed. When cool, pipe melted semisweet chocolate onto tops of cookies.
Maple-Walnut Packages: Cut out rolled-out Maple Walnut Cookie dough with 2 1/2 x 1 3/4-inch rectangular cutter. Place on cookie sheet. Bake as directed. When cool, frost with blue-tinted Vanilla Glaze. Decorate with star sprinkles. Pipe on a green-tinted White Icing "ribbon."
Almond Ice-Box Slices: Shape chilled Almond Cookie dough into 12-inch roll. Wrap and chill until very firm. Cut into 1/4-inch-thick slices. Place on cookie sheet. Bake as directed. When cool, dip half in melted semisweet chocolate.

One delicious dough, spiced and iced, yields many delights. To turn basic vanilla cookie dough into seven varieties, follow our simple switches or try add-ins. Then roll, press, or slice into the shapes shown here — or others to suit your fancy. (Clockwise from top) Ginger-cinnamon Spice Kids, tangy Lime Slices, Lemon Blossoms, Mint Candy Canes, Choco-Orange Bull's-Eyes, Maple-Walnut Packages, and chocolate-dipped Almond Ice-Box Slices.

HOLIDAY NUT DROPS

- **1 1/2 cups all-purpose flour**
- **1/2 teaspoon baking soda**
- **1/2 teaspoon salt**
- **3/4 cup packed light-brown sugar**
- **1/2 cup (1 stick) butter, at room temperature**
- **1 egg**
- **1 teaspoon vanilla**
- **1 cup chopped unsalted mixed nuts**
- **1/2 cup mini red and green candy-coated chocolate pieces**

1. Heat oven to 350°. Lightly grease 2 baking sheets. Mix together flour, baking soda, and salt in a bowl.
2. Beat brown sugar and butter in another bowl until creamy and smooth, about 2 minutes. Beat in egg and vanilla. Stir in flour mixture. Fold in nuts and chocolate pieces. Drop by rounded measuring tablespoonfuls, 2 inches apart, onto prepared baking sheets.
3. Bake in 350° oven for 10 to 12 minutes or until lightly browned at edges. Let cool slightly on baking sheets. Transfer to wire rack to cool. Store in airtight container.
Yield: Makes 2 dozen cookies.

Chocolate-Peanut Cookies and Holiday Nut Drops (right) *make for a tower of can't-say-no treats. Fruit Crescents* (above) *are Italian-style sugar cookies with a super surprise inside — fabulous dried-fruit filling of figs, dates, raisins, and pine nuts.* (Opposite, from left) *A twist of lemon and a cup of grated pecans go into classic British Lemon Rounds; inside, a creamy lemon-curd filling. Cardamom-laced dough enfolds a crunchy filling of walnuts, apricot preserves, and cinnamon in perky Swedish Pinwheels.*

CHOCOLATE-PEANUT COOKIES

Prepare Holiday Nut Drops dough, reducing salt to 1/4 teaspoon. Add 2 squares (1 ounce each) unsweetened chocolate, melted, along with egg. Replace mixed nuts and candy with 1 cup honey-roasted peanuts, chopped, and 1/2 cup white-chocolate baking chips. Drop level measuring tablespoons batter onto baking sheets. If desired, arrange 5- to 6-pointed star of peanut halves on top of each cookie; you will need another 1/2 to 2/3 cup peanuts. Bake in 350° oven for 10 to 12 minutes. Cool on wire rack. Store in airtight container.
Yield: Makes 32 cookies.

FRUIT CRESCENTS

- **3 1/2 cups all-purpose flour**
- **1 tablespoon baking powder**
- **1/2 teaspoon salt**
- **3/4 cup (1 1/2 sticks) unsalted butter, at room temperature**
- **3/4 cup sugar**
- **1 egg**
- **1 teaspoon vanilla**
- **1/4 cup milk**
- **3/4 cup dried figs, chopped**
- **3/4 cup pitted dates, chopped**
- **1/2 cup pine nuts (pignoli)**
- **1/4 cup dark seedless raisins**
- **1 teaspoon ground cinnamon**
- **1/4 cup orange juice**
- **1 egg, lightly beaten**
- **Multicolor decor balls**

1. Combine flour, baking powder, and salt in bowl. Beat butter and sugar in large bowl until creamy. Beat in egg and vanilla until fluffy. Stir in flour mixture and milk. Divide dough into fourths; flatten into disks. Wrap in plastic. Refrigerate 30 minutes.
2. For filling, pulse figs, dates, pine nuts, raisins, cinnamon, and juice in food processor until chopped.
3. Heat oven to 350°. Coat 2 baking sheets with nonstick vegetable-oil cooking spray.
4. On lightly floured surface with floured rolling pin, roll one dough piece into 9 x 6-inch rectangle. Cut into nine 3 x 2-inch pieces. Place heaping teaspoon filling lengthwise down center of each piece. Fold long sides to meet in center; pinch to seal. Place, seam-side down, on prepared sheets. Shape into crescents. Cut 3 slits into top of each

cookie with scissors or knife. Brush lightly with beaten egg. Sprinkle with multicolor balls. Repeat with remaining dough and filling.
5. Bake in 350° oven for 25 minutes or until cookies are lightly golden. Remove to wire racks to cool. Store at room temperature or freeze.
Yield: Makes 3 dozen cookies.

LEMON ROUNDS

- **2 1/2 cups all-purpose flour**
- **1/2 teaspoon salt**
- **1/2 teaspoon baking soda**
- **3/4 cup plus 1 cup sugar**
- **1 cup plus 6 tablespoons (2 3/4 sticks) unsalted butter, at room temperature**
- **1 egg**
- **1 teaspoon lemon extract**
- **1 teaspoon vanilla**
- **1 cup finely ground pecans**
- **1/2 cup lemon juice**
- **2 teaspoons grated lemon zest**
- **2 egg yolks**
- **Confectioners' sugar**

1. Combine flour, salt, and baking soda in medium bowl. Beat 3/4 cup sugar and 1 cup butter in large bowl until creamy. Beat in egg and extracts until fluffy. Stir in flour mixture and pecans. Divide dough in half; shape into disks. Wrap in plastic wrap. Refrigerate 1 hour.
2. Heat oven to 350°. On lightly floured surface with floured rolling pin, roll half of dough to 1/8-inch thickness. With floured 3-inch fluted round cookie cutter, cut out dough. Place 1 inch apart on ungreased baking sheets. With floured 1 1/2-inch round cookie cutter, cut out centers from half the cookies. Reroll scraps. Repeat with other half of dough.
3. Bake in 350° oven for 12 to 15 minutes or until lightly browned. Cool on racks. Store at room temperature or freeze.
4. For curd, combine 1 cup sugar and 6 tablespoons butter, lemon juice, and zest in saucepan. Place pan in skillet half-filled with simmering water over medium-low heat. Whisk in yolks. Cook, stirring, until thickened enough to coat spoon, 15 minutes (temperature should read 160°); do not boil. Pour into small bowl; cover surface directly with plastic wrap. Refrigerate to chill, 2 hours.
5. Sprinkle confectioners' sugar on cookies with cutout centers. Spread 1 tablespoon curd over each solid cookie; top with sugared cutout cookie, pressing lightly to form sandwich.
Yield: Makes 16 cookies.

SWEDISH PINWHEELS

- **2 cups all-purpose flour**
- **2 teaspoons ground cardamom**
- **1/2 teaspoon salt**
- **1/2 cup (1 stick) unsalted butter, at room temperature**
- **2/3 cup sugar**
- **1 egg**
- **1 teaspoon vanilla**
- **1 cup chopped walnuts**
- **1/4 cup apricot preserves**
- **1 teaspoon ground cinnamon**
- **1 tablespoon sugar**
- **1 egg white, lightly beaten**
- **Red and green sugars**

1. Heat oven to 325°. Combine flour, cardamom, and salt in medium bowl. Beat butter and 2/3 cup sugar in large bowl until creamy. Beat in egg and vanilla until fluffy. Stir in flour mixture. Divide dough into thirds; flatten into disks. Wrap separately in plastic. Refrigerate 1 hour.
2. Combine walnuts, apricot preserves, cinnamon, and 1 tablespoon sugar in small bowl. Set aside. Grease 2 large baking sheets.
3. On floured surface with floured rolling pin, roll one third of dough into 9-inch square. Keep unused dough refrigerated. Cut dough into nine 3-inch squares. Place squares 1 inch apart on prepared sheets. With small knife, cut four 1 3/4-inch-long slits into each square, from each corner almost to center. Spoon 1 teaspoon filling onto center of each square; brush edges with egg white.
4. Fold every other tip over filling past center; press lightly to stick. Place additional 1/4 teaspoon filling on top of center tips. Brush tops with egg white; sprinkle with colored sugars. Repeat with remaining dough and filling.
5. Bake in 325° oven for 12 minutes or until lightly golden. Cool cookies on wire racks. Store at room temperature or freeze.
Yield: Makes 27 cookies.

christmas dinner

YOU CAN SERVE UP THE PERFECT HOLIDAY FEAST WITH THESE FABULOUS SELECTIONS. JUST ADD FRESH SALAD, ROLLS, AND SATISFYING BEVERAGES.

Menu

Fresh Green Salad (toss your own or pick up ready-to-serve)

Standing Rib Roast with Fennel Crust • Baked Garlic Potatoes

Sliced Tomatoes Provençale • Broccoli and Cauliflower with Cheese Sauce

Tender Rolls (homemade or from the bakery, served oven-warm)

Orange-Cream Carrot Cake with golden raisins and coconut

STANDING RIB ROAST WITH FENNEL CRUST

- **1 rib roast (9 pounds, about 4 ribs), trimmed and chine removed**
- **2 cloves garlic, chopped**
- **1 teaspoon salt**
- **1 tablespoon fennel seeds, crushed**
- **2 teaspoons dried thyme**
- **2 teaspoons ground black pepper**
- **2 teaspoons olive oil**

Shallot-Wine Sauce:

- **1 can (13¾ ounces) beef broth**
- **½ cup dry red wine**
- **2 tablespoons finely chopped shallots**
- **2 tablespoons all-purpose flour**
- **½ teaspoon dried thyme**
- **¼ teaspoon salt**
- **1 tablespoon browning-and-seasoning sauce (optional)**

A majestic Standing Rib Roast and a medley of side dishes will win a standing ovation. Our twice-baked potatoes (bottom) are laced with garlic and Parmesan cheese. A drizzling of Cheddar tops the tender Broccoli and Cauliflower with Cheese Sauce (recipe on next page).

1. Heat oven to 450°. Place roast in large roasting pan.
2. Carefully mash together garlic and ½ teaspoon salt with side of knife to make paste; place in bowl. Stir in fennel, thyme, pepper, oil, and remaining salt. Spread over top of roast.
3. Roast beef in 450° oven for 15 minutes. Reduce temperature to 350°. Roast until instant-read meat thermometer inserted in thickest part without touching bone registers 120°, about another 2 hours. Let roast stand 20 minutes.
4. Prepare Shallot-Wine Sauce: Pour pan drippings into a 2-cup measure. Set roasting pan aside. Skim 2 tablespoons of fat from drippings and place in a 2-quart saucepan. Skim any remaining fat from drippings and discard. Add broth and wine to roasting pan. Place pan over medium-high heat; stir up any browned bits from bottom of pan with wooden spoon; add to drippings in measuring cup.
5. Add shallots to fat in saucepan; cook until softened, 3 minutes. Stir in flour, thyme, and salt until smooth. Gradually whisk in drippings. Cook, stirring, until sauce boils and thickens. Remove from heat. Stir in browning sauce, if using.
6. Carve roast. Serve with sauce.
Yield: Makes 16 servings.

BAKED GARLIC POTATOES

- **2 whole heads garlic**
- **3 tablespoons olive oil**
- **6 large baking potatoes (about 3½ pounds), scrubbed**
- **⅔ cup chicken broth**
- **¾ teaspoon salt**
- **½ teaspoon ground white pepper**
- **3 tablespoons shredded Parmesan cheese**
- **Paprika**

1. Heat oven to 425°.
2. Rub garlic with ½ teaspoon olive oil. Wrap each head loosely in aluminum foil. Pierce each potato in several places with fork.
3. Bake potatoes and garlic in 425° oven for 50 minutes or until potatoes are knife-tender and garlic is soft to the touch. Keep oven on.
4. Halve each potato lengthwise. Scoop out pulp into large bowl. Reserve 8 potato shells (use other 4 shells for potato skins). Unwrap garlic; cut heads of garlic in half horizontally. Squeeze garlic pulp from papery skins into bowl with potatoes; discard garlic skins. Add chicken broth, remaining olive oil, salt, and pepper to potato mixture. Mash with potato masher until smooth and creamy. Spoon back into 8 reserved potato shells. Sprinkle with Parmesan cheese and paprika.
5. Bake in 425° oven for 10 minutes longer or until tops are golden brown.
Yield: Makes 8 servings.

BROCCOLI AND CAULIFLOWER WITH CHEESE SAUCE

- 1 large head cauliflower
- 1 large head broccoli
- 2 teaspoons salt

Cheddar Cheese Sauce:

- 3 tablespoons butter
- 3 tablespoons all-purpose flour
- 1 teaspoon dry mustard
- 1½ cups milk
- 1 8-ounce block sharp Cheddar cheese, shredded (about 2 cups)
- ¼ teaspoon hot-pepper sauce

1. Cut cauliflower into flowerets. Cut tough stalks from broccoli; trim tough sides; cut stalks into "coins"; cut head into flowerets.
2. Bring 6 cups water in large saucepan to boiling. Add cauliflower, broccoli, and salt. Return to boiling; cook, stirring occasionally, until vegetables are tender-crisp, about 8 minutes. Drain.
3. Meanwhile, prepare the sauce. Melt butter in a 2-quart saucepan over medium heat. Whisk in flour and mustard until smooth; cook for 1 minute. Gradually stir in milk until smooth. Bring to boiling. Remove saucepan from heat. Stir in cheese and hot-pepper sauce, stirring until cheese is melted. Spoon sauce over vegetables.
Yield: Makes 8 servings.

SLICED TOMATOES PROVENÇALE

- 4 large tomatoes (2½ pounds)
- ¾ teaspoon salt
- 3 slices white bread, torn in pieces
- ¼ cup grated Parmesan cheese
- 2 tablespoons chopped fresh parsley
- 1 tablespoon olive oil
- 1 clove garlic, finely chopped
- ½ teaspoon dried leaf oregano, crumbled
- ½ teaspoon ground black pepper

1. Heat oven to 475°.
2. Slice each tomato into 4 equal slices, each about ¾ inch thick. Place the slices in a single layer on a large ungreased baking sheet. Sprinkle the tomatoes with ½ teaspoon salt.
3. Place bread in food processor or blender. Pulse with on/off motion until fine crumbs form.
4. Combine the bread crumbs, Parmesan cheese, chopped parsley, olive oil, garlic, oregano, pepper, and the remaining ¼ teaspoon salt in a small bowl. Sprinkle evenly over the tomato slices.
5. Bake tomatoes in 475° oven for 15 minutes or until tender and topping is golden. Serve hot or at room temperature.
Yield: Makes 8 servings.

Sliced Tomatoes Provençale are sprinkled with flavored bread crumbs and baked until golden. (Opposite) *For dessert, golden raisins and fragrant coconut enrich this Orange-Cream Carrot Cake. Edge with wisps of orange and crunchy walnut halves.*

ORANGE-CREAM CARROT CAKE

Carrot Cake:

3 cups finely shredded carrots (3 to 4 large)
1 cup shredded fresh coconut OR sweetened coconut
1/2 cup golden raisins
2 cups all-purpose flour
2 teaspoons baking soda
1 teaspoon ground cinnamon
1/2 teaspoon baking powder
1/2 teaspoon salt
1/4 teaspoon ground allspice
1/4 teaspoon ground nutmeg
1/4 cup honey
1/2 cup lightly packed light-brown sugar
1 cup low-fat plain yogurt
1/2 cup vegetable oil
2 eggs
2 egg whites
1 teaspoon vanilla

Orange-Cream Frosting:

1 cup (2 sticks) butter or margarine, at room temperature
1/2 teaspoon salt
2 boxes (1 pound each) confectioners' sugar
4 to 6 tablespoons orange juice
3 tablespoons grated orange zest
4 small oranges
16 walnut halves (optional)

1. Heat oven to 350°. Grease two 9-inch round layer-cake pans.

2. Prepare Carrot Cake: Mix together carrots, coconut, and raisins in medium bowl.

3. Combine flour, baking soda, cinnamon, baking powder, salt, allspice, and nutmeg in large bowl.

4. Whisk honey, brown sugar, yogurt, oil, eggs, egg whites, and vanilla in medium bowl until well blended. Add to flour mixture, whisking together until smooth. Add carrot mixture, stirring just until well combined.

5. Divide mixture evenly between prepared pans.

6. Bake in 350° oven for 35 minutes or until wooden pick inserted in center comes out clean. Remove pans to wire racks; cool 10 minutes. Invert cakes onto racks to cool completely.

7. Prepare Orange-Cream Frosting: Beat together butter and salt in small bowl until fluffy. Beat in confectioners' sugar alternately with orange juice until smooth and spreadable. Fold in orange zest.

8. Place 1 cake layer on cake plate. Spread frosting over top. Place second layer on top of first. Spread frosting over sides and top of cake.

9. To decorate cake, thinly slice 1 orange. Fold orange slices in half; arrange on top of cake with walnut halves, if you wish. Remove zest (outer, colored part of peel, with no bitter white pith) from remaining orange with swivel-bladed vegetable peeler. Cut zest into thin strips; scatter on top.

Yield: Makes 10 servings.

a moveable feast

WHAT BETTER WAY TO RING IN THE SEASON THAN A ROUND-ROBIN PARTY? DIFFERENT FAMILIES PREPARE APPETIZERS, DINNER, AND DESSERT SO THE JOB — AND THE JOY! — ARE SHARED.

TIP: *To make certain everything goes smoothly and the dishes all coordinate, appoint one family as the "host."*

1ST HOUSE
Cheese Toasts
Mushroom-Filled Double Pinwheels
Taco Dip and Chips
Mini Crab Cakes
Herb-and-Spice-Coated Cheese Balls

2ND HOUSE
Salad with Buttermilk Dressing
Tomato-Rosemary Chicken
Mushroom Rice • Make-Ahead Rolls

3RD HOUSE
Holiday Trifle • Bourbon Balls
Apple Tart • Key Lime Cheesecake

CHEESE TOASTS

- **4 slices bacon, chopped, cooked until crispy, and drained**
- **1/3 cup chopped pitted black olives**
- **2 tablespoons chopped chives**
- **2 teaspoons chopped fresh parsley**
- **1/4 cup mayonnaise**
- **1 teaspoon Worcestershire sauce**
- **Dash hot-pepper sauce**
- **12 slices party rye bread**
- **1 cup shredded Swiss cheese**

1. Heat oven to 375°.
2. Mix bacon, olives, chives, parsley, mayonnaise, Worcestershire, and pepper sauce; spread on bread. Top with cheese.
3. Bake on baking sheet in 375° oven for 10 minutes to melt cheese. Cut into triangles. Serve immediately.
Make-Ahead Tip: Mix mayonnaise; grate cheese day ahead; refrigerate.
Yield: Makes 24 triangles.

MUSHROOM-FILLED DOUBLE PINWHEELS

- **5 tablespoons butter**
- **18 ounces fresh mushrooms (your choice of variety), finely chopped**
- **2 cups finely chopped onion**
- **2 tablespoons all-purpose flour**
- **1 1/2 teaspoons dried thyme**
- **1/2 teaspoon salt**
- **1/4 teaspoon ground black pepper**
- **1 teaspoon fresh lemon juice**
- **1 1/2 packages (17 1/4 ounces each) frozen puff pastry (3 sheets), thawed according to package directions**
- **1 large egg, lightly beaten**
- **1 tablespoon water**

1. Heat butter in large skillet over medium heat. Add mushrooms and onion; cook, stirring, 13 minutes or until liquid evaporates and mushrooms are tender. Stir in flour, thyme, salt, pepper, and lemon juice. Cook, stirring, for 2 minutes or until thickened. Let cool.
2. Unfold 1 pastry sheet on lightly floured work surface. Spread one-third of mushroom mixture evenly to edge of pastry. Starting on a short side, roll up to center. Do the same on the other side; lightly press sides together. Cover; chill 1 hour. Repeat with remaining 2 pastry sheets and mushroom mixture.
3. Heat oven to 400°.
4. Cut chilled pastry crosswise into 1/4-inch-thick slices, about 32 slices per roll. Place, cut side down, 1 inch apart on ungreased baking sheets. Stir egg and water in small bowl. Brush slices with egg wash, without letting wash drip down sides.
5. Bake in 400° oven for 15 minutes or until golden. Serve warm.
Make-Ahead Tip: Unbaked, uncut, filled rolls can be refrigerated a day ahead; then cut and bake, Steps 4 and 5 above, 15 to 18 minutes. Or unbaked rolls can be frozen up to 3 weeks, then thawed in refrigerator, and cut and baked as above.
Yield: Makes 8 dozen.

Allow about an hour for the first course, where guests can mingle and munch bite-size treats. Start with Cheese Toasts enriched with bacon (opposite) *and crispy Mushroom-Filled Double Pinwheels* (this page).

TACO DIP AND CHIPS

- 1 container (8 ounces) whipped cream cheese
- 1 package (1.25 ounces) taco seasoning
- 1 cup medium-hot bottled salsa
- 1/4 head lettuce, separated into leaves
- 1 large tomato, seeded, chopped, and drained on paper toweling
- 1 medium-size onion, chopped
- 1 cup shredded Cheddar cheese
- Tortilla chips

Mix the cream cheese, taco seasoning, and 2 tablespoons salsa in a bowl. Spread over the bottom of a large serving platter. Top with the remaining salsa. Then layer lettuce, tomato, onion, and Cheddar over salsa. Serve with chips.

Make-Ahead Tip: Make cream cheese mixture a day ahead and refrigerate, covered.

Yield: Makes 8 servings.

HERB-AND-SPICE-COATED CHEESE BALLS

Coriander-Cumin Cheese Balls:

- 1/3 cup finely chopped coriander (cilantro), parsley, or watercress
- 1 teaspoon ground cumin
- 1 pound Jarlsberg cheese
- 1 tablespoon melted butter or margarine

Gingered-Sesame Cheese Balls:

- 1/3 cup sesame seeds, toasted (see Note)
- 1 1/4 teaspoons ground ginger
- 1 1/4 teaspoons soy sauce
- 1 pound mozzarella cheese
- 1 tablespoon melted butter or margarine

Paprika-Pistachio Cheese Balls:

- 4 teaspoons finely ground pistachio nuts
- 2 1/2 teaspoons paprika
- 1 pound Cheddar cheese

1. Prepare Coriander-Cumin Cheese Balls: Mix coriander and cumin in small bowl until well blended; set aside.

2. Using a 3/4 or 7/8-inch melon baller, scoop out balls of cheese from wedge of Jarlsberg. Save scraps for snacks.

3. With wooden pick, dip a cheese ball into melted butter, letting excess liquid drip off.

4. Sprinkle coriander-cumin mixture over entire ball, patting to help coating adhere. Place on a platter. Cover and refrigerate until ready to serve.

5. Prepare Gingered-Sesame Cheese Balls: Mix sesame seeds, ginger, and soy sauce in small bowl until well blended; set aside. Proceed as in Steps 2 and 3 using mozzarella cheese and butter. (Use sesame-ginger mixture in Step 4.)

6. Prepare Paprika-Pistachio Cheese Balls: Mix ground nuts and paprika in small bowl. Proceed as in Steps 2 and 3 using Cheddar cheese and omitting melted butter. (Substitute paprika mixture for coating in Step 4.)

Yield: Makes 6 dozen cheese balls.

Note: Toast sesame seeds in small heavy skillet over medium heat until lightly golden, about 2 minutes.

MINI CRAB CAKES

- 1 sweet red pepper, coarsely chopped
- 2 green onions, coarsely chopped
- 1/2 pound surimi, cut up OR lump crabmeat, picked over to remove bits of cartilage
- 1 celery rib, cut up
- 1 teaspoon Dijon-style mustard
- 1/4 teaspoon hot-pepper sauce
- 6 slices thin-sliced white bread, torn in small pieces
- 3 eggs
- 1/2 teaspoon Worcestershire sauce
- 1/2 cup dry plain bread crumbs
- 6 cups vegetable oil, for frying
- Cajun Mayonnaise (recipe follows)

1. Place red pepper, onions, surimi, celery, mustard, pepper sauce, bread, eggs, and Worcestershire in food processor. Pulse to chop. Refrigerate 15 minutes to allow bread to absorb any liquid.

2. Place dry plain bread crumbs on piece of waxed paper.

3. Shape rounded tablespoons of surimi mixture into 1 1/2-inch balls. Roll ball in bread crumbs; flatten slightly into thick patty. Place on baking sheet. Refrigerate for 15 minutes.

4. Heat oil in deep-fat fryer or large skillet until temperature reaches 375°. Fry 6 cakes at a time until golden brown, 1 to 1 1/2 minutes. Remove cakes with slotted spoon to paper toweling to drain. Serve warm with Cajun Mayonnaise.

Cajun Mayonnaise: Whisk 1 cup mayonnaise, 1 tablespoon ketchup, 1 teaspoon Dijon-style mustard, 1/2 teaspoon hot-pepper sauce, and 1/2 teaspoon Worcestershire sauce in a small bowl. Refrigerate, covered, up to 2 days.

Make-Ahead Tip: These mini crab cakes can be cooked ahead, cooled thoroughly, wrapped airtight, and frozen. To serve, thaw in the refrigerator. Place in a single layer in shallow baking pan. Bake in 350° oven until heated through, about 10 minutes.

Yield: Makes 24 mini crab cakes.

MAKE-AHEAD ROLLS

2 packages active dry yeast
1¾ cups warm water (105° to 115°)
½ cup sugar
1 teaspoon salt
1 egg, slightly beaten
¼ cup (½ stick) butter, at room temperature
5½ cups all-purpose flour
½ cup grated Parmesan cheese
2 tablespoons dried minced onion
⅛ teaspoon ground red pepper
1 tablespoon butter, melted

1. Sprinkle yeast over warm water in bowl. Add sugar and salt. Stir to dissolve completely.
2. Add egg, butter, and 3 cups flour. Beat at high speed 2 minutes. Gradually add cheese, onion, and red pepper. Stir in 1 cup flour.
3. Turn dough out onto surface. Knead until smooth and elastic, working in flour as needed to prevent sticking. Place in large bowl. Brush top with melted butter. Cover with plastic wrap. Let rise in refrigerator until doubled in bulk, 2 hours.
4. Punch dough down. Refrigerate 1 to 3 days; punch down each day. Bake rolls all at once, or one batch a day for 3 days.
5. For dozen rolls: Remove third of dough from refrigerator; let stand at room temperature 2 hours. On floured surface, roll into 12-inch-long rope; cut in 12 pieces. Shape each piece into ball; tuck underneath to make smooth top. Place ½-inch apart in greased round 8- or 9-inch round cake pan. Cover with towel; let rise in warm place until doubled in bulk, 30 to 45 minutes.
6. Heat oven to 375°.
7. Bake in 375° oven for 15 to 20 minutes or until golden brown. Brush with melted butter, if desired.
Yield: Makes 3 dozen.

SALAD WITH BUTTERMILK DRESSING

1 cup buttermilk
¼ cup sour cream
¼ cup mayonnaise
1 teaspoon chopped shallots
1 teaspoon cider vinegar
1 teaspoon sugar
½ teaspoon salt
¼ teaspoon garlic powder
12 to 14 cups lightly packed mixed salad greens (about 1 pound)

Whisk buttermilk, sour cream, mayonnaise, shallots, vinegar, sugar, salt, and garlic powder in bowl. Refrigerate up to 2 days. Toss greens with half the dressing to coat. Pass remaining dressing.
Yield: Makes 12 servings.

As visiting gets underway, bring out Taco Dip and Chips (opposite), *along with Herb-and-Spice-Coated Cheese Balls* (not shown). *Serve Mini Crab Cakes* (above, left) *with Cajun-style mayo for dipping. To accompany the main entrée, drizzle crisp salad greens with Buttermilk Dressing. Oven-fresh Make-Ahead Rolls* (not shown) *get extra zing from Parmesan cheese and onion flakes.*

An entrée of baked Tomato-Rosemary Chicken served with savory Mushroom Rice is a sure winner with diners of all ages.

TOMATO-ROSEMARY CHICKEN

- **12 boneless, skinned chicken breast halves (about 4 pounds total)**
- **1/2 teaspoon salt**
- **1/4 teaspoon ground black pepper**
- **1/4 cup all-purpose flour**
- **2 tablespoons vegetable oil**
- **2 tablespoons butter**
- **5 cloves garlic, chopped**
- **1/4 pound piece prosciutto, chopped**
- **1/3 cup dry white wine**
- **1 tablespoon chopped fresh rosemary OR 1 teaspoon dried rosemary, crushed**
- **12 plum tomatoes, diced**
- **1/2 cup chicken broth**

1. Season both sides of chicken breasts with salt and pepper. Place flour on sheet of waxed paper. Dip chicken in flour to coat both sides; shake off any excess flour and place chicken on another piece of waxed paper.
2. Heat oven to 375°.
3. Heat 1 tablespoon oil and 1 tablespoon butter in a large nonstick skillet over medium-high heat.
4. Add 6 chicken breasts to skillet; sauté until lightly browned, about 3 minutes per side. Place chicken in 15 1/2 x 10 1/2 x 1-inch baking pan in single layer. Repeat with remaining oil, butter, and chicken.
5. Bake chicken in 375° oven for 20 minutes or until no longer pink in center.
6. Meanwhile, add garlic and prosciutto to skillet; cook over medium heat, stirring constantly, for 3 minutes. Add wine and rosemary; cook, stirring up any browned bits from bottom of skillet, for 2 minutes.
7. Add tomatoes and broth. Bring to boiling. Reduce heat; simmer 10 minutes.
8. Place chicken on serving platter; pour sauce over top. Serve immediately.

Make-Ahead Tip: In Step 5, bake chicken until just cooked through, about 15 minutes. Refrigerate immediately, covered. Refrigerate cooled sauce from Step 7, covered. To serve, reheat chicken in baking pan, uncovered, in 325° oven for about 10 minutes. Gently reheat sauce in saucepan.
Yield: Makes 12 servings.

MUSHROOM RICE

- **1/2 ounce dried porcini mushrooms**
- **Warm water, as needed**
- **3/4 cup uncooked wild rice**
- **2 tablespoons butter**
- **1 medium-size onion, chopped**
- **1 teaspoon chopped fresh rosemary OR 1/2 teaspoon dried rosemary, crushed**
- **1 cup shredded carrots**
- **3 cups uncooked white rice**
- **3 cans (13 3/4 ounces each) chicken broth plus enough water to make 6 cups**
- **1/2 teaspoon ground black pepper**
- **1/4 cup chopped fresh parsley**

1. Cover dried mushrooms in small bowl with warm water. Let stand 10 minutes, until softened. Drain; rinse; squeeze out excess water from mushrooms. Chop finely.
2. Combine wild rice and enough water in saucepan to keep rice well covered. Bring to boiling. Lower heat; simmer, uncovered, until rice is tender and individual grains have opened, 45 to 50 minutes. Add water as needed to keep rice covered. Drain; keep warm.
3. Heat butter in large, deep nonstick skillet or saucepan over medium heat. Add onion, rosemary, mushrooms, and carrots; cook, stirring, 6 minutes or until vegetables are softened. Add white rice, broth, and pepper. Bring to boiling. Lower heat; cover; simmer 20 minutes, until rice is tender. Drain excess liquid.
4. Mix wild rice, white rice, and parsley in bowl. Serve hot.
Yield: Makes 12 servings.

HOLIDAY TRIFLE

- 2 all-butter pound cakes (12 ounces each), cut into 1-inch cubes
- 1 can (5 ounces) evaporated milk
- 1 can (14 ounces) sweetened condensed milk
- 2 cups heavy cream, whipped OR 4 cups frozen nondairy whipped topping, thawed
- 1 cup shredded sweetened coconut
- Raspberries, for garnish (optional)

1. Arrange half the cake cubes in bottom of 3- to 4-quart straight-sided glass bowl.

2. Combine evaporated milk and condensed milk in small bowl. Pour half the milk mixture over cake cubes in bowl. Spread with whipped cream or topping. Sprinkle with half the coconut. Repeat layering with remaining ingredients. Chill at least 1 hour or overnight. Garnish with berries, if desired.

Yield: Makes 16 servings.

Dazzling do-ahead treats are the grand finale. The Holiday Trifle, featuring chunks of pound cake and dollops of whipped cream, tastes as great as it looks.

After dinner, luscious Bourbon Balls (below) will prove irresistible. Our Apple Tart (opposite, top) has a rich cream cheese filling. Key Lime Cheesecake has zesty flavor.

BOURBON BALLS

- 2½ cups finely crushed vanilla wafers (about 10 ounces)
- 1¼ cups confectioners' sugar
- 2 tablespoons finely ground hazelnuts
- ¼ cup bourbon
- 2 tablespoons unsweetened cocoa powder
- 3 tablespoons corn syrup
- ⅓ cup granulated sugar

1. Mix crumbs, confectioners' sugar, hazelnuts, bourbon, cocoa, and corn syrup in medium-size bowl.
2. Press all ingredients in bowl together to form a large ball.
3. Shape into balls, 1 tablespoon for each; place on waxed paper.
4. Place granulated sugar in small shallow dish. Roll small balls in sugar to coat. Place in tightly covered container at least 24 hours for flavors to develop.
Make-Ahead Tip: Store in tightly covered container in cool place up to several weeks.
Yield: Makes about 2 dozen.

APPLE TART

Pastry:

- ½ cup (1 stick) butter, at room temperature
- ⅓ cup sugar
- ½ teaspoon vanilla
- 1 cup all-purpose flour

Filling:

- 1 package (8 ounces) cream cheese, at room temperature
- ¼ cup sugar
- 1 egg
- ½ teaspoon vanilla

Apple Topping:

- ¼ cup sugar
- ½ teaspoon ground cinnamon
- 4 cups peeled and sliced apples
- 3 tablespoons apple jelly, melted
- Sweetened whipped cream and cinnamon, for garnish (optional)

1. Prepare Pastry: Beat butter, sugar, and vanilla in bowl until smooth and creamy. On low speed, beat in flour. Shape into a ball. Press pastry over the bottom of a 9-inch springform pan and 2 inches up sides.
2. Prepare Filling: Beat cream cheese and sugar in small bowl until light and fluffy. Beat in egg and vanilla until blended, about 1 minute. Spread evenly over pastry.
3. Heat oven to 450°.
4. Prepare Apple Topping: Combine sugar and cinnamon in bowl. Add sliced apples; toss to coat. Arrange apple slices in circular pattern on cream cheese mixture.
5. Bake in 450° oven for 10 minutes. Reduce heat to 400°. Bake 25 minutes or until apples are tender and lightly golden. Brush with jelly. Transfer to rack to cool. Refrigerate to chill. Remove side of pan. Serve tart with sweetened whipped cream with dusting of cinnamon, if desired.
Make-Ahead Tip: Make tart a day ahead; refrigerate in tart pan.
Yield: Makes 8 servings.

KEY LIME CHEESECAKE

Crust:

- 3 cups graham cracker crumbs
- ⅔ cup sugar
- ⅔ cup butter, melted

Filling:

- 1 cup fresh lime juice
- ¼ cup water
- 2 envelopes unflavored gelatin
- 1½ cups sugar
- 5 eggs, slightly beaten
- 2 teaspoons grated lime zest
- ½ cup (1 stick) butter, at room temperature
- 2 packages (8 ounces each) cream cheese, at room temperature
- ½ cup heavy cream, chilled
- Whipped cream and lime slices, for garnish (optional)

1. Prepare Crust: Stir crumbs, sugar, and melted butter in bowl. Press over bottom of 9-inch springform pan and up sides.
2. Prepare Filling: Combine lime juice and water in saucepan; sprinkle gelatin over top. Let stand 5 minutes to soften. Stir sugar, eggs, and zest into pan. Cook, stirring, over medium heat until almost boiling, about 7 minutes or until instant-read thermometer reaches 160°; do not let boil. Remove from heat.
3. Beat butter and cream cheese in large bowl until well mixed, 1 minute. Gradually beat in lime mixture until well blended. Refrigerate, stirring, until mixture thickens enough to mound slightly when dropped from spoon, about 45 minutes.
4. Beat chilled cream in small chilled bowl until stiff peaks form. Fold into lime mixture. Pour into prepared crust. Cover; refrigerate until firm, 3 to 4 hours.
5. Run thin knife around inside of pan to loosen sides; remove side of pan. Garnish with whipped cream and lime slices, if desired. Store in refrigerator.
Yield: Makes 16 servings.

dazzling DESSERTS

HOMEMADE INDULGENCES ALWAYS DELIVER TWO REWARDS. THERE'S THE FUN OF PUTTERING IN AN AROMA-FILLED KITCHEN — AND LATER, THE JOY OF SHARING THE SCRUMPTIOUS RESULTS.

GINGERBREAD CAKE

- 1/2 cup molasses
- 3/4 cup boiling water
- 1 teaspoon baking soda
- 2 1/4 cups all-purpose flour
- 1 teaspoon baking powder
- 2 teaspoons ground cinnamon
- 1/2 teaspoon ground cloves
- 1/2 teaspoon salt
- 10 tablespoons (1 1/4 sticks) butter or margarine, softened
- 1 1/4 cups sugar
- 2 eggs
- Orange-Cream-Cheese Frosting (recipe follows)
- Orange zest and raspberries for garnish (optional)

1. Heat oven to 350°. Grease and flour two 8-inch (6-cup) straight-sided layer-cake pans.
2. Combine molasses, boiling water, and baking soda in 2-cup glass measure; this will bubble up. Mix flour, baking powder, cinnamon, cloves, and salt on waxed paper.
3. Beat butter and sugar in bowl until light and fluffy. Beat in eggs, one at a time, beating well after each addition. Alternately stir in flour mixture and molasses mixture, beginning and ending with flour.
4. Bake in 350° oven for 25 minutes. Cool in pans on wire rack 10 minutes. Remove cakes from pans to rack to cool completely.
5. With serrated knife, cut cakes horizontally in half. Place one layer on serving platter, cut side up. Frost top with about 2/3 cup Orange-Cream-Cheese Frosting. Repeat with remaining layers. Refrigerate until serving time. Garnish with orange zest and raspberries.

Orange-Cream-Cheese Frosting: Beat 8 ounces low-fat cream cheese, softened, and 1/4 cup (1/2 stick) butter or margarine, softened, in bowl until creamy. Gradually beat in 1-pound box confectioners' sugar until well blended and smooth. Beat in 2 teaspoons grated orange zest. If frosting is too soft, cover and refrigerate until desired consistency.
Yield: Makes 14 servings.

CASHEW-CARAMEL CLUSTERS

- 25 caramel candies
- 1 tablespoon water
- 2 cups unsalted cashews
- 1/2 cup milk-chocolate chips
- 1/3 cup chopped white baking chocolate

1. Spray baking sheet with nonstick vegetable-oil cooking spray. In double boiler, combine caramels and water. Cook, stirring, until smooth.
2. Stir in cashews until coated; drop by teaspoonfuls onto prepared baking sheets.
3. Melt chocolate chips and baking chocolate separately over low heat, stirring until smooth. Spoon each into separate plastic food-storage bags. Seal; squeeze each chocolate to corner. Snip corner of each bag; drizzle chocolates over candies. Let stand until firm.
Yield: Makes 32 candies.

Molasses, cinnamon, and ground cloves meld wonderfully in our layered Gingerbread Cake (opposite) *with orange-cream-cheese frosting.* (This page) *Make Cashew-Caramel Clusters ahead; store them in airtight containers for up to three weeks.*

CHOCOLATE CREAM PIE

Use a pastry mix for single-crust pie.

Chocolate Filling:

- **1/2 cup sugar**
- **2 tablespoons cornstarch**
- **1 envelope unflavored gelatin**
- **1/4 teaspoon salt**
- **2 cups milk**
- **4 egg yolks**
- **1 teaspoon vanilla**
- **6 ounces semisweet chocolate, chopped**

Topping:

- **1 cup heavy cream**
- **2 tablespoons confectioners' sugar**
- **1 teaspoon vanilla**
- **Chocolate curls (optional)**

Airy puffs of whipped cream and a flaky crust complement an ultra-rich Chocolate Cream Pie.

1. Prepare piecrust mix for single-crust pie following package directions, use purchased refrigerated crust, or make your favorite recipe.
2. Roll out crust on floured surface to 12-inch circle. Transfer to 9-inch pie plate. Trim pastry, leaving 1-inch overhang. Fold overhang under; pinch to form stand-up edge; crimp. Cover with plastic wrap; refrigerate 1 hour.
3. Heat oven to 400°.
4. Remove plastic wrap; line pastry with aluminum foil, gently easing foil into corners. Fill with dried beans, uncooked rice, or pie weights.
5. Bake in 400° oven for 15 minutes. Remove foil and rice or beans. Bake crust for 10 minutes longer or until golden. Cool completely on wire rack.
6. Prepare Chocolate Filling: Combine sugar, cornstarch, gelatin, and salt in heavy, medium-size saucepan. Stir in milk. Cook, stirring constantly, over medium heat until mixture thickens. Remove saucepan from the heat.
7. Stir egg yolks lightly in medium-size bowl. Stir in small amount of milk mixture. Slowly pour yolk mixture back into milk mixture, stirring with wire whisk to prevent lumping. Return saucepan to heat. Cook over low heat, stirring constantly, for about 2 minutes or until mixture is very thick; do not let boil. Remove saucepan from heat. Add chocolate and stir until chocolate is melted. Pour filling into cooled crust. Place plastic wrap directly on surface of filling. Refrigerate for 2 hours or until the filling is thoroughly chilled.
8. Prepare Topping: Combine heavy cream, sugar, and vanilla in medium-size bowl. Beat with hand mixer on medium speed until soft peaks form. Spoon on top of pie. Scatter chocolate curls over the top of the pie, if desired.
Yield: Makes 12 servings.

GIFT-BOX CAKES

- **2 1/2 cups all-purpose flour**
- **4 teaspoons baking powder**
- **1/2 teaspoon salt**
- **3/4 cup unsalted butter**
- **2 cups sugar**
- **3 eggs**
- **2 teaspoons vanilla**
- **1 1/4 cups milk**

Chocolate Glaze:

- **3/4 pound semisweet baking chocolate, chopped**
- **1 1/2 cups heavy cream**
- **34 large nonpareil candies**
- **88 small nonpareil candies (1/3 cup)**
- **Ribbon, for decoration**

1. Heat oven to 350°. Line 13 x 9 x 2-inch baking pan with waxed paper; spray with nonstick vegetable-oil cooking spray. Cover 5-inch square of cardboard with aluminum foil.
2. In large bowl, stir together flour, baking powder, and salt. In another large bowl, cream butter with electric mixer until smooth. Beat in sugar, eggs, and vanilla until light and fluffy. On low speed, alternately beat in milk and the flour mixture in thirds, mixing just until blended.

3. Scrape into prepared pan. Bake in 350° oven for 30 to 35 minutes or until wooden pick inserted in center comes out clean. Cool cake in pan on wire rack for 10 minutes. Invert cake onto rack and cool completely. Remove waxed paper, and trim cake level, if needed.
4. Measuring from long side, cut two $5^1/_4$-inch square layers from cake for larger box (base of stack). Cut four $2^1/_4$-inch square layers from remaining piece for 2 smaller boxes.
5. Prepare Chocolate Glaze: In food processor, chop chocolate very finely. In saucepan, heat cream until bubbles appear around edges. With motor running, add hot cream to chocolate in steady stream. Process until mixture is smooth. Scrape $^1/_2$ cup of the chocolate into small bowl; scrape remaining chocolate into medium bowl.
6. Place the small bowl over ice water, and let stand, stirring occasionally, until mixture achieves soft-frosting consistency, about 15 minutes. Place 1 large cake layer on foil-lined cardboard. Frost tops of 1 large and 2 small layers. Top each with matching layer to form 3 box shapes.
7. Place large wire cooling rack over waxed paper. Place boxes on rack. Let remaining glaze stand at room temperature, stirring occasionally, until it resembles texture of thin sour cream, about $1^1/_2$ to 2 hours. Spoon glaze over sides of each box, spreading with spatula, if needed, to coat. Spoon on top, and spread level. Reuse any glaze that has dripped off boxes and reapply it, if needed.
8. Attach large nonpareils onto sides of large box, as pictured. Attach small nonpareils on sides and tops of both small boxes, as pictured. Let boxes stand at room temperature until glaze is set. Place large box on serving plate. Place 1 of small boxes on top of large box, in center. Arrange large nonpareils around top of large box.

9. Cut 2 strips of ribbon to go over cake stack. Make bow with ribbon. Place 2 strips, crossing, in center, and attach bow. Place over cake, cutting off any excess ribbon and tucking in at base of cake. Serve with smaller gift cake (not pictured).
Yield: Makes 12 servings.

Unwrap our Gift-Box Cakes — they're iced with chocolate glaze and dotted with nonpareils large and small. Inside, buttercream joins moist white-cake layers.

Frost the nutty Cranberry Cake Wreath with a sugar glaze, and pipe on pine boughs. For a merry finish, add a bright-red bow. (Opposite) Our marvelous Peppermint Ice-Cream Roll, glazed with chocolate and topped with crushed candy cane, will "wow" your guests — but assembly is easy with step-by-step instructions.

CRANBERRY CAKE WREATH

Cake:

- **3 cups all-purpose flour**
- **1½ cups sugar**
- **2 teaspoons baking powder**
- **½ teaspoon baking soda**
- **¾ teaspoon salt**
- **3 eggs**
- **¾ cup orange juice**
- **½ cup (1 stick) unsalted butter, melted**
- **1 cup fresh or frozen, thawed cranberries**
- **1 cup coarsely chopped walnuts (4 ounces)**

Glaze:

- **3 to 4 teaspoons milk**
- **2 cups confectioners' sugar**
- **Green paste food coloring**
- **Cinnamon red-hot candies OR cranberries, for garnish (optional)**

1. Heat oven to 350°. Grease and flour 12-cup ring mold or Bundt pan.
2. Combine flour, sugar, baking powder, baking soda, and salt in large bowl. Make a well in center. Add eggs, orange juice, and butter to well; stir into dry ingredients just until blended.
3. Add cranberries and walnuts to well. Stir together liquid and dry ingredients just until combined. Spread batter in prepared pan.
4. Bake in 350° oven for 45 to 50 minutes or until wooden pick inserted in center comes out clean. Cool cake in pan on wire rack 10 minutes. Remove wreath from pan; cool completely.
5. Prepare Glaze: Gradually stir milk into confectioners' sugar until smooth. Spread top of cake with 1 cup of the glaze. Tint remaining 1 cup glaze with green paste food coloring. (If glaze is too thin for piping, stir in a little more confectioners' sugar.) Spoon tinted glaze into pastry bag fitted with small round tip. Pipe on pine branches as pictured. Decorate with candies or cranberries and red bow, if you wish.
Yield: Makes 12 servings.

PEPPERMINT ICE-CREAM ROLL

Cake:

- **¾ cup all-purpose flour**
- **¼ cup unsweetened cocoa powder**
- **1 teaspoon baking powder**
- **¼ teaspoon salt**
- **4 eggs**
- **¾ cup granulated sugar**
- **¼ cup milk**
- **1 teaspoon vanilla**
- **1 tablespoon confectioners' sugar mixed with 1 tablespoon unsweetened cocoa powder**
- **3 cups vanilla ice cream**
- **¼ teaspoon peppermint extract**
- **¼ cup crushed candy canes**

Chocolate Glaze:

- **6 squares (1 ounce each) semisweet chocolate, chopped OR 1 cup chocolate morsels**
- **⅔ cup heavy cream**
- **⅛ teaspoon peppermint extract (optional)**
- **6 or 7 chopped red and white peppermint candies**

1. Prepare Cake: Heat oven to 375°. Grease 15 x 10 x 2-inch sheet pan; line with waxed paper; grease paper.
2. Sift together flour, cocoa powder, baking powder, and salt into medium-size bowl.
3. Beat eggs in medium-size bowl until lemon colored, about 5 minutes. Gradually beat in granulated sugar until well blended. Beat in milk and vanilla. Fold in flour mixture. Scrape into prepared pan.
4. Bake in 375° oven for 12 to 15 minutes or until cake springs back when lightly touched.
5. Meanwhile, spread clean cloth towel on work surface. Sift confectioners' sugar-cocoa powder mixture onto towel. When cake is done, invert onto dusted towel. Remove pan and waxed paper. Starting at a short end, roll up towel with cake inside. Place on wire rack and let cool completely.
6. Soften ice cream in medium-size bowl. Beat in peppermint extract and crushed candy canes. Line 13 x 9 x 2-inch pan with plastic wrap. Spread ice cream into plastic-lined pan. Freeze for 15 to 20 minutes.
7. Once cake has cooled and ice cream is firm, but pliable, unroll cake. Invert ice cream onto cake, leaving 1½-inch border on a short end. Spread ice cream slightly with rubber spatula to edges of cake, leaving the border. Using towel as a guide and starting at the short end of the cake with the border, carefully roll up cake with ice-cream filling inside. Place on wire rack in large pan in freezer.
8. Prepare Chocolate Glaze: Place chocolate in medium-size bowl. Bring cream just to simmering in small saucepan. Pour over chocolate in bowl; stir until mixture is smooth, adding peppermint extract, if using. Let cool slightly, 3 to 5 minutes or until it registers 85° on instant-read thermometer. Meanwhile, in plastic bag, finely crush the peppermint candies with a heavy saucepan or rolling pin.
9. Pour glaze over cake roll, using a spatula if necessary to spread evenly over the roll. Sprinkle the top of the roll with the crushed candies. Place in freezer 4 hours or overnight until frozen. To serve, let stand at room temperature to soften slightly, about 10 minutes.
Yield: Makes 12 servings.

FROZEN TRIPLE-CHOCOLATE TERRINE

Bittersweet Chocolate Layer:

- **3 tablespoons unsalted butter**
- **6 ounces bittersweet chocolate, chopped**
- **1 tablespoon coffee liqueur**
- **1/2 cup heavy cream, whipped**

White Chocolate Layer:

- **3/4 teaspoon unflavored gelatin**
- **1 tablespoon water**
- **3/4 cup heavy cream**
- **4 ounces white chocolate baking squares, chopped**

Milk Chocolate Layer:

- **8 ounces milk chocolate, chopped**
- **1 tablespoon hazelnut liqueur**
- **1/2 cup heavy cream**
- **1 tablespoon unsweetened cocoa powder**
- **Shaved white chocolate and unsweetened cocoa powder, for garnish (optional)**

1. Coat 8 x 4 x 2-inch loaf pan lightly with nonstick vegetable-oil cooking spray. Line with plastic wrap, smoothing out major wrinkles. Fill another loaf pan about three-quarters full with dried beans. Wedge loaf pan into beans so pan is tilted lengthwise.

2. Prepare Bittersweet Layer: Melt butter in small saucepan. Add chocolate, stirring until smooth. Stir in liqueur; cool. Fold in whipped cream. Pour into loaf pan, smoothing top with icing spatula; the top of mousse should form a diagonal across the pan. Place pans in freezer until mousse is firm, about 45 minutes.

3. Prepare White Chocolate Layer: Soften gelatin in water in small cup, 5 minutes. Heat together 1/4 cup cream and gelatin mixture in small saucepan to a bare simmer, stirring. Remove from heat. Stir in white chocolate until smooth. Let stand just until cool to touch, but still fluid.

4. Beat remaining 1/2 cup heavy cream in bowl until stiff peaks form. Fold into white chocolate mixture. Pour into tilted loaf pan; spread evenly. Freeze until firm, 30 minutes.

5. Prepare Milk Chocolate Layer: Melt chocolate in small saucepan over low heat, stirring until smooth. Remove from heat. Stir in liqueur. Let stand just until cool to the touch, but still fluid. Beat heavy cream in bowl until stiff peaks form. Fold cream into chocolate mixture.

6. Remove terrine from beans and place on flat surface. Pour in milk chocolate mixture; spread level. Cover and refrigerate until firm, about 2 hours. (Terrine can be frozen for up to 1 month.)

7. To serve: For easy slicing, freeze terrine for 1 hour. Unmold. Cut into thin slices. Transfer to dessert plates. If desired, garnish with shaved white chocolate and a dusting of unsweetened cocoa powder forced through a fine-mesh sieve.

Yield: Makes 16 servings.

This Frozen Triple-Chocolate Terrine combines white, milk, and bittersweet chocolate…all meltingly good. (Opposite) Score big with showy Neapolitan Christmas Cake, inspired by the striped ice-cream block of the same name.

NEAPOLITAN CHRISTMAS CAKE

- **1 cup cake flour (not self-rising)**
- **1/2 cup ground almonds**
- **1 teaspoon baking powder**
- **1/4 teaspoon salt**
- **8 egg whites (about 1 cup)**
- **1/4 teaspoon cream of tartar**
- **3/4 cup granulated sugar**
- **1/4 teaspoon almond extract**
- **Green and red food coloring**
- **1 3/4 cups heavy cream**
- **1 teaspoon unflavored gelatin**
- **3 tablespoons confectioners' sugar**
- **1/4 cup strawberry jam**
- **3/4 cup sweetened flake coconut**

1. Heat oven to 350°. With nonstick vegetable-oil cooking spray, coat three 9 1/4 x 5 1/4 x 2 3/4-inch loaf pans. Line with waxed paper.

2. Mix flour, almonds, baking powder, and salt in a bowl.

3. Beat egg whites and cream of tartar in large bowl until foamy. Gradually add granulated sugar, beating until stiff peaks form. Sprinkle half the flour mixture over whites; fold in gently. Repeat with remaining flour. Fold in almond extract.

4. Measure 1 1/4 cups batter into each of 2 separate bowls. Tint 1 light green, other pink. Transfer pink batter into one pan, green batter into second, remaining white into third.

5. Bake in 350° oven for 12 minutes, until tops spring back when pressed. Invert onto racks; peel off paper. Cool.

6. Heat 1/4 cup cream and gelatin in saucepan; stir to dissolve. Cool.

7. Beat remaining cream and confectioners' sugar in bowl until slightly thickened and frothy. Add gelatin mixture. Beat to stiff peaks.

8. Place green layer on platter. Spread with half the jam. Top with 1/2 cup cream mixture. Sprinkle with 1/4 cup coconut. Continue layering with white cake, remaining jam, 1/2 cup cream mixture, and 1/4 cup coconut. Top with pink layer. Frost top and sides of cake with cream mixture. Place remaining coconut in plastic bag with 1 drop of green food coloring; knead to blend color. Sprinkle cake with tinted coconut. Refrigerate cake 45 minutes or until whipped cream is firm.

Yield: Makes 10 servings.

SPICED EGGNOG CHEESECAKE

Crust:

- **8 boards graham crackers**
- **1 teaspoon sugar**
- **1/4 teaspoon ground ginger**
- **1/4 teaspoon ground nutmeg**
- **1/4 teaspoon ground cinnamon**
- **1/4 cup (1/2 stick) butter, melted**

Filling:

- **4 packages (8 ounces each) cream cheese, at room temperature**
- **3/4 cup sugar**
- **1/4 cup all-purpose flour**
- **1/4 teaspoon ground nutmeg**
- **1/4 teaspoon ground cinnamon**
- **Pinch ground cloves**
- **1 egg**
- **1 3/4 cups prepared eggnog (with or without alcohol)**
- **1 teaspoon vanilla**
- **1 container (8 ounces) sour cream**

Garnish (optional):

- **1 package (6 ounces) premium white chocolate baking bars**
- **Pinch ground nutmeg**

1. Heat oven to 350°.
2. Prepare Crust: Crush crackers in plastic bag. Add sugar, ginger, nutmeg, and cinnamon. Add butter; knead bag to blend. Press over bottom of 9-inch round springform pan.
3. Bake crust in 350° oven for 10 minutes. Cool on wire rack.
4. Prepare Filling: Beat cream cheese in bowl until smooth. Mix sugar, flour, nutmeg, cinnamon, and cloves in small bowl. Add to cream cheese; beat until smooth. Beat in egg. Beat in eggnog in slow stream. Beat in vanilla. Pour into springform pan; tap pan lightly to release air bubbles.
5. Bake in 350° oven for 1 hour. Remove from oven; spread with sour cream. Bake 5 more minutes. Cool in pan on rack until cool to touch. Refrigerate until serving.
6. Optional Garnish: Melt chocolate in bowl over saucepan of simmering water. Add nutmeg. Line 8 x 4 x 3-inch loaf pan with foil. Pour chocolate into pan, spreading evenly; cool until firm. Lift out of pan. Make curls, using vegetable peeler. Arrange on top of cake.
Yield: Makes 12 servings.

CARAMEL APPLE PIE CUPS

- **3 Granny Smith apples (about 2 pounds), peeled, cored, and chopped**
- **3/4 cup firmly packed light-brown sugar**
- **3 tablespoons butter**
- **1/4 cup apple juice**
- **1/4 cup heavy cream**
- **1/4 teaspoon apple pie spice**
- **1 tablespoon cornstarch**
- **1/4 cup soft caramels (about 8 pieces), unwrapped**
- **2 boxes (11 ounces each) piecrust mix**
- **1/2 to 2/3 cup cold water**

1. Combine apples, brown sugar, butter, apple juice, cream, pie spice, cornstarch, and caramels in a skillet. Bring to boiling over high heat, stirring frequently, 8 to 10 minutes. Lower heat to medium; cook for another 2 to 3 minutes or until slightly thickened and fruit is tender. Remove from heat.
2. Heat oven to 425°.
3. Stir together 2 boxes piecrust mix and cold water in medium-size bowl until dough comes together in ball. Divide in half. Transfer half of dough to floured work surface. Roll out to 1/8- to 1/4-inch thickness. Using 4-inch round cutter or lid of 13-ounce coffee can, cut out 6 circles. Then with 2 3/4-inch cutter, cut 6 smaller circles, rerolling scraps as needed (see Note). Repeat with second half of dough, cutting out six 4-inch circles and six 2 3/4-inch circles. Reserve any leftover dough for other uses, refrigerating for up to 3 days, or freezing up to 1 month.
4. Press a 4-inch circle of dough into a 2 3/4 x 2-inch cup of a muffin tin, pressing dough up sides. Repeat with remaining large circles and cups, filling a total of 12 cups.
5. Fill each pastry-lined cup with a scant 1/4 cup filling. Top pie bottoms with smaller circles.
6. Bake in 425° oven for 15 minutes or until crust is golden and filling is bubbly. Remove pies to wire rack to cool. Serve with vanilla ice cream, if desired.
Note: Decoratively pierce tops, use small cookie cutter to cut out designs in tops, or cut small circles into strips for lattice tops.
Yield: Makes 12 pie cups.

One bite of Spiced Eggnog Cheesecake (opposite) *will delight the taste buds.* (This page) *In less than half an hour, you can transform packaged piecrust into adorable Caramel Apple Pie Cups.*

a christmas welcome (pages 6-11)

NORTH STAR

You need: 2"-thick white plastic foam, two sheets 12" x 36"; felt-tip marker; serrated knife; glue gun; white statice, baby's breath, acadia/mimosa foliage; green sheet moss; newspaper; silver glitter spray paint; U-pins; picture wire; wreath hanger.
Making pattern: On a copier, enlarge half star (below) to 28"W; cut out.
Cutting foam: Place pattern on one foam sheet with dashed line at one long edge. Trace pattern with marker. (***Note:*** Plastic foam will be too narrow to accommodate point at opposite side. Trim excess foam from between points; hot glue excess to extend foam to fit pattern.) Cut out star with knife. Repeat. Glue half stars together.
Preparing baby's breath: Cover work area with newspaper; spray baby's breath with glitter; let dry.
Decorating: ***Statice*** – Cut sprigs 3"L. Insert all over star. ***Baby's breath*** – For center of star, cut sprigs 6"L to 8"L; insert in center. For points of star, cut sprigs 3"L to 4"L; insert in points. ***Acadia*** – Tuck in random sprigs in center of star. ***Moss*** – Cut sheet moss to fit along edges; attach with U-pins.
Adding hanger: Stretch wire across back of star, securing it with U-pins. Hang star on door with wreath hanger.

RUSTIC WELCOME PLAQUE (continued)

Finishing: For hanger, nail two nails at top back of plaque 18" apart. Tie string around nails. Hang plaque on door. Glue red ribbon bows to wreath; hang wreath. Hang some cones from nails on front of plaque, using nails or glue to secure. Arrange additional cones on plaque shelf.

DELLA ROBBIA DOORWAY

You need: Artificial fruit – apples, pears, peaches, grapes, 2 pineapples; wooden floral picks; floral wire; artificial cedar, gold mistletoe, berries; 2 artificial spiral trees; glue gun; 2 1/2"W gold and sheer plaid wired ribbons; two 9'L artificial evergreen garland.
Preparing items: Attach wooden floral picks or lengths of wire to each fruit piece. Cut cedar, mistletoe, and berries into 6" to 9" lengths.
Decorating each tree: Wire fruit along the boughs of tree, saving pineapple for tree topper. Insert cedar, mistletoe, and berry sprigs among branches, using glue to secure if needed. Wire ends of 1 yd lengths of ribbon to floral picks. Secure ribbon lengths to tree with picks, arranging attractively. Tie a bow using both ribbons. Wire bow and a pineapple to top of tree.
Making each door spray: Cut three 24" lengths of garland. Lay lengths side by side and wire together 9" from one end. Wire fruit, mistletoe, and berries to greenery. Tie a ribbon bow. Wire ribbon bow to swag.

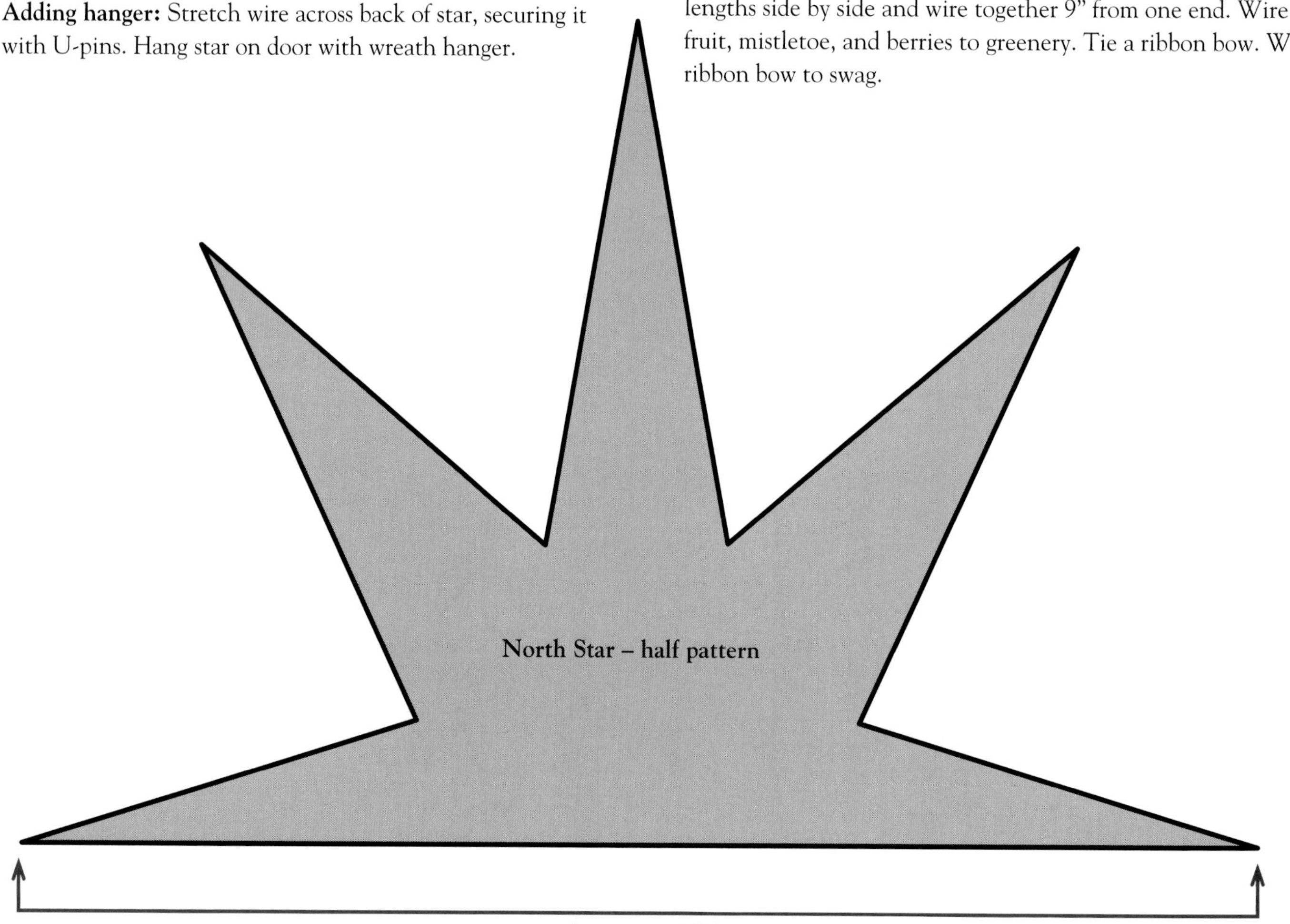

Decorating swag: Glue mistletoe to second garland. Tie one bow with long streamers. Wire bow to center of swag.
Finishing: Attach swag above door. Secure sprays to each door. Place a tree on each side of entrance.

FABULOUS FLORAL WREATH

You need: Newspaper; dried materials – hydrangea, seeded eucalyptus, scabiosa, mini pinecones, seed pods, echinacea cones; spray paint – gold, silver; 22" dia. plastic foam wreath form; wreath hanger; gauzy bow.
Making wreath: Cover work area with newspaper. Choose materials to spray-paint gold or silver as desired. When dry, gather clusters of like materials; insert in wreath. Arrange so colors are varied. Repeat until full.
Finishing: Hang on door with wreath hanger. Tack or tape (decorative-only) bow above.

ALL-GREEN WREATH

You need: 22-gauge green floral wire; dried eucalyptus; fresh boxwood branches; euonymus branches; cocculus leaves; 14" dia. plastic foam wreath form.
Making wreath: Cut wire into 12" pieces. Wrap wire around clusters of eucalyptus, boxwood branches, euonymus branches and cocculus leaves. Insert large branch clusters into wreath form in overlapping clockwise layers. Insert leaf clusters into wreath form, filling any empty spaces between layers of branches.
Finishing: Cut 18" of wire; fold in half lengthwise. Twist ends together to form hanging loop. Twist end of loop around top of wreath.

Plaque Base Diagram

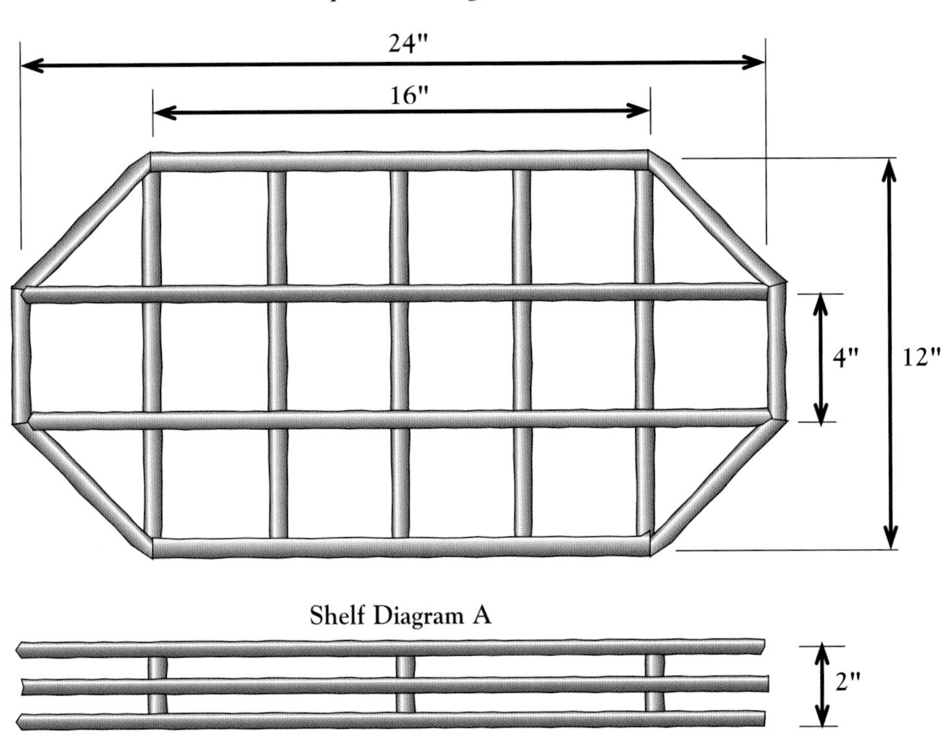

Shelf Diagram B

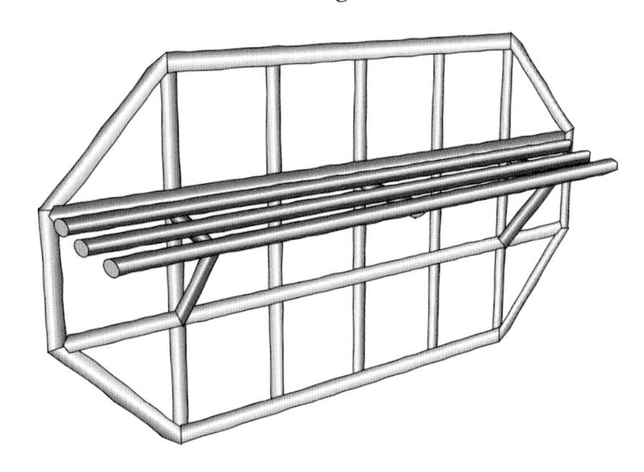

retro regalia (pages 12-21)

ADVENT CALENDAR

You need: $1^1/_2$ yds Christmas-print fabric; 1 yd red felt; $^1/_4$ yd cream cotton fabric; numbered stamp set; black ink pad; pinking shears; 10 yds of $^1/_8$"W cream ribbon; perle cotton – green, cream; 2 white buttons; red jingle bells; fabric glue.
Stamping: Stamp numbers 1 through 25 on cream fabric. Using pinking shears, cut out each number.
Cutting: From felt, cut twenty-five 2" x $2^1/_2$" pockets. From Christmas fabric, cut two 24" x 20" pieces for calendar front and back.
Decorating pockets: Pin a number on each pocket. Using perle cotton, embroider numbers onto pockets as desired. Sew ribbon around outer edges of pockets 1-13, 17, 18 and 22-24. Refer to photo (page 12) to cut overflaps for pockets 14, 16, 19, 21 and 25. Embroider edges of each flap as desired. Pin flap behind each pocket. Using pinking shears, cut diagonally across centers of two remaining pockets to make openings. Cut two 4" pieces of ribbon; fold each in half to make loops. Stitch ends of loops to upper back edge of pockets 17 and 22. Fold down loops; stitch button to front of pockets in center of each loop.
Assembling: Arrange pockets on calendar front, evenly spaced; machine-stitch pockets to front. From felt, cut two 19" x 1" pieces and two 23" x 1" pieces for frame. Glue frame to front, placing frame pieces $^1/_2$" in from edges of front. Sew ribbon to frame edges. Pin front to back, with right sides facing. Stitch edges in $^1/_2$" seams, leaving opening along one edge. Trim corners; turn. Slipstitch opening closed.

SNOW DOLLS

You need: 2 yds antique white plush felt; fiberfill stuffing; 2 white $^3/_8$" buttons; 4 black beads; felt – $^1/_4$ yd each of red, green, black; fabric glue; 27" x $4^1/_2$" piece of plaid wool fabric; small silk holly clusters; chalk pencil; black embroidery floss; double-sided self-adhesive cardboard; metallic silver paper; 4 self-adhesive hook-and-loop fastener circles; metal file; 4 large nails.
Cutting: Enlarge patterns (page 121). From plush felt, cut four head sections, two body front sections, two body back sections, four arm sections and one nose for each doll.
Sewing each doll: (***Note:*** All stitching is done in $^1/_4$" seams, with right sides facing and raw edges even, unless noted.) Pin and stitch each pair of head sections together along one curved edge to make head front and back. Pin head front to head back; stitch along curved edge. Pin and stitch body front sections together along center front seam. Pin and stitch body back sections together along center back seam, leaving opening in center of seam. Pin and stitch body front to body back along all edges. Pin and stitch each pair of arm sections together along curved edges, leaving short end open. Turn each section right side out. Stuff body; slipstitch opening closed. Stuff arms, leaving upper $^1/_2$" unstuffed. Slipstitch arms to top of body. Stuff head; turn under $^1/_4$" on lower edge. Pin and slipstitch head to body, over ends of arms. Sew gathering stitches along edge of nose. Place button in center; pull up threads to gather. Knot thread ends together. Glue nose to doll. Sew bead eyes to doll. Draw mouth on doll. Stitch mouth using black floss and satin stitches.
Making boy's scarf: Pull threads at each short end of plaid fabric to form fringe; tie around neck.
Making girl's scarf: Cut one $13^1/_2$" x $4^1/_2$" piece each of red and green felt. Sew pieces together on one short end. Cut short ends in scallops; tie around neck.
Making boy's hat: From black felt, cut two $6^3/_4$" circles for brim, one $7^1/_2$" x $2^1/_4$" piece for crown and one $2^1/_4$" circle for top. Cut slit in center of one brim. Pin and stitch brims together along outer edge; turn right side out through slit. Topstitch edges. Roll crown section crosswise to form tube; glue edges. Stitch crown in center of brim. Stuff crown; glue remaining circle on top of crown. Glue holly clusters to brim. Glue hat on head.
Making girl's hat: From red felt, cut one crown, one 4" circle for top of hat, and one 1" x 12" strap. From green felt, cut one cuff. Fold crown in half crosswise: pin and stitch short ends together. Pin and stitch circle to one end of crown; turn. Fold cuff in half crosswise; pin and stitch short ends together. Pin and stitch right side of cuff to wrong side of lower edge of hat. Turn cuff to right side of hat. Glue one end of strap inside one side of hat. Glue hat on head. Glue other end of strap inside other side of hat; trim excess.
Making skis: Cut four $6^3/_4$" x $^3/_4$" strips of cardboard and four $7^3/_4$" x $1^3/_4$" pieces of silver paper. Remove backing from cardboard; press silver paper onto cardboard and wrap excess to wrong side. Curl up one end of each piece to form skis. Separate hook-and-loop fastener circles. Attach loop portions to center bottoms of feet. Attach hook portions to centers of skis.
Making ski poles: File off pointed end of each nail; glue to each hand.

1 square = 1"

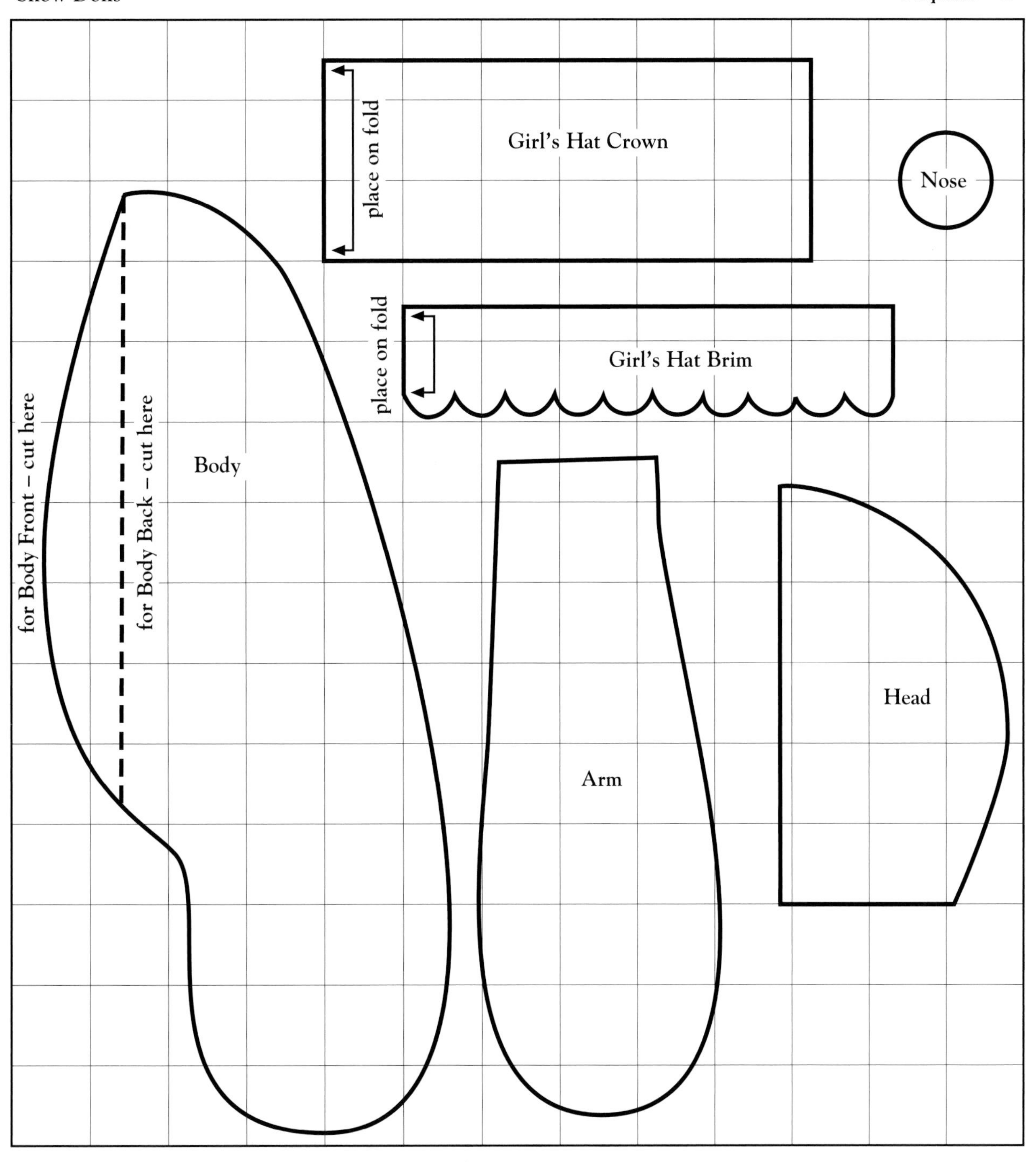

place on fold
Girl's Hat Crown
Nose
place on fold
Girl's Hat Brim
for Body Front – cut here
for Body Back – cut here
Body
Head
Arm

PONY ORNAMENTS

You need (for each): 1/4 yd printed cotton fabric; remnant of contrasting fabric; fiberfill stuffing; 4 1/2" x 1" piece of cardboard; skein of yarn; 2 moving doll eyes; fabric glue.

Cutting: Use full-sized patterns (below and page 123). From print fabric, cut two body sections, two underside sections, and two ear sections. From contrasting fabric, cut two ears.

Sewing: (***Note:*** All stitching is done in 1/4" seams, with right sides facing and raw edges even, unless noted.) Pin and stitch underside sections together along long straight edge, leaving opening in center. Pin and stitch body sections together along upper edge between marks. Pin and stitch underside to body, matching seams to marks. Clip curves; turn right side out. Stuff firmly; slipstitch opening closed.

Making mane: Wrap yarn crosswise around cardboard, covering cardboard completely. Hand-stitch along one long edge to form mane; slip mane off cardboard. Pin to pony's head; slipstitch mane to pony.

Making tail: Wrap yarn lengthwise around cardboard about 20 times. Hand-stitch along one short edge to form tail; slip tail off cardboard. Cut loops open at unstitched end. Pin and hand-stitch tail to back of pony.

Making ears: Glue each print ear to contrast ear, with wrong sides together. Fold each ear in half along straight edge; glue to head.

Finishing: Glue eyes to head.

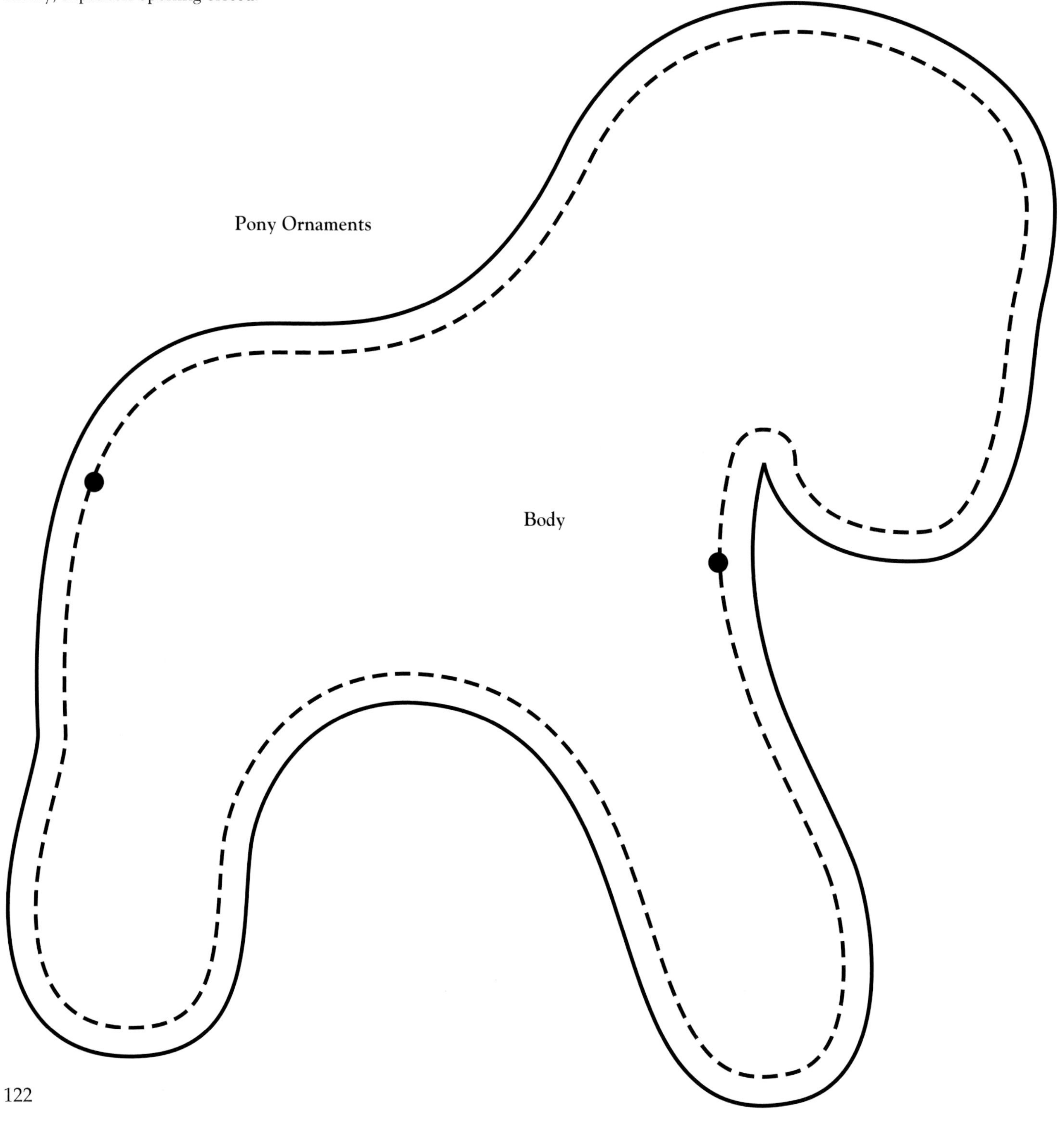

FABRIC GLOBES

You need: Assorted plastic foam balls, 1" to 4" across; fabric remnants; flat-head pins; colored sisal cord; matching paper twist ribbon; glue gun.
Making balls: Cut fabrics into ½"W strips. Wrap strips around balls; pin ends in place.
Finishing large balls: Cut 10" of cord and 5" of paper twist for each ball. Fold each cord in half; knot ends to make hanging loop. Untwist paper; tie around loop, just below knot, to make bow. Pin bow to top of ball; secure with drop of glue.
Finishing small balls: Cut 8" of cord for each ball; tie in bow. Pin bow to top of ball; secure with drop of glue.

HANKIE PILLOWS

You need (for each): Square Christmas-print handkerchief; ¾ yd checked or striped fabric; 2 yds of 1"W coordinating ribbon; fiberfill stuffing.
Cutting: Measure handkerchief. Add 3½" all around. Cut two pieces of fabric to this measurement for pillow front and back.
Assembling: Pin handkerchief to center of front piece, right side up. Pin ribbon around edges of handkerchief, folding in fullness at corners. Stitch close to both edges of ribbon. Pin front to back, right sides facing and raw edges even. Stitch edges in ½" seams, leaving an opening along one side. Trim corners; turn. Stuff. Slipstitch opening closed.

BOW-TRIMMED BOOTIE (continued)

Finishing: Cut 6" of ribbon; fold in half to form hanging loop. Hand-stitch hanging loop inside upper back corner of stocking. Starting at seam, hand-stitch ribbon to lower edge of cuff. Cut remaining ribbon into two equal pieces; tie each piece in bow. Layer bows; stitch through all layers at center. Sew double bow to cuff.

LINEN CUFF STOCKING

You need: ½ yd of red print fabric; remnant of embroidered linen; ½ yd of lace trim; ¼ yd of narrow cord; about 16 wood beads in Christmas colors.
Cutting: Enlarge pattern (page 124). From red fabric, cut two stocking sections for front and back. From linen, cut one 14" x 3¼" cuff, centering embroidery in one half of cuff.
Sewing: (***Note:*** All stitching is done in ¼" seams, with right sides facing and raw edges even, unless noted.) Pin and stitch front to back along sides and lower edges, leaving upper edge open. Clip curves; turn. Turn under ¼" on one long edge of cuff; press. Pin trim under pressed-under edge; stitch close to fold to trim cuff. Fold cuff in half crosswise; stitch short ends together. Turn. Slip cuff inside upper edge of stocking. Pin and stitch untrimmed edge of cuff to upper edge of stocking, aligning seams. Fold cuff to right side of stocking.
Finishing: String beads onto cord; knot ends together to form hanging loop. Hand-stitch loop inside upper back corner of stocking.

Pony Ornaments

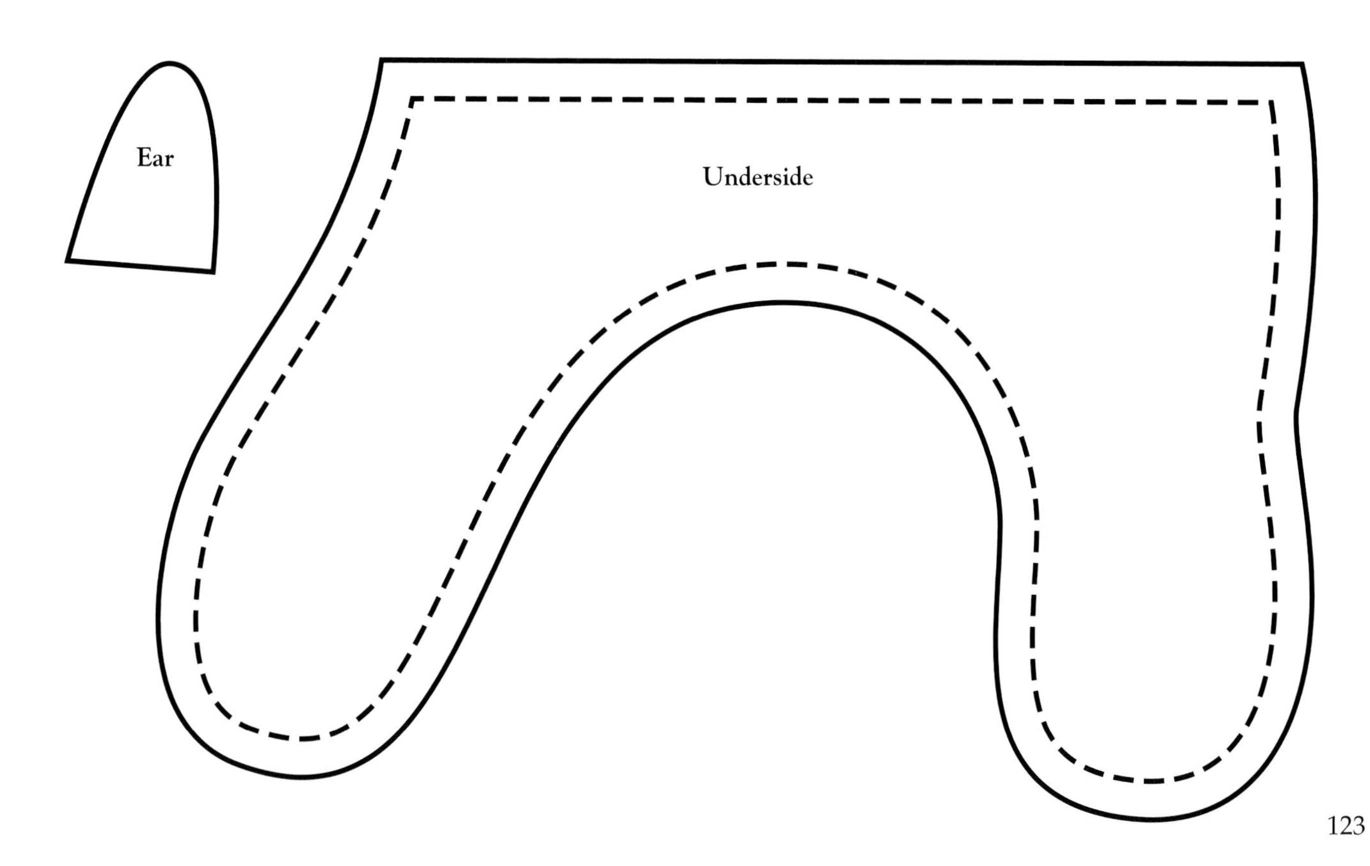

Linen Cuff Stocking

1 square = 1"

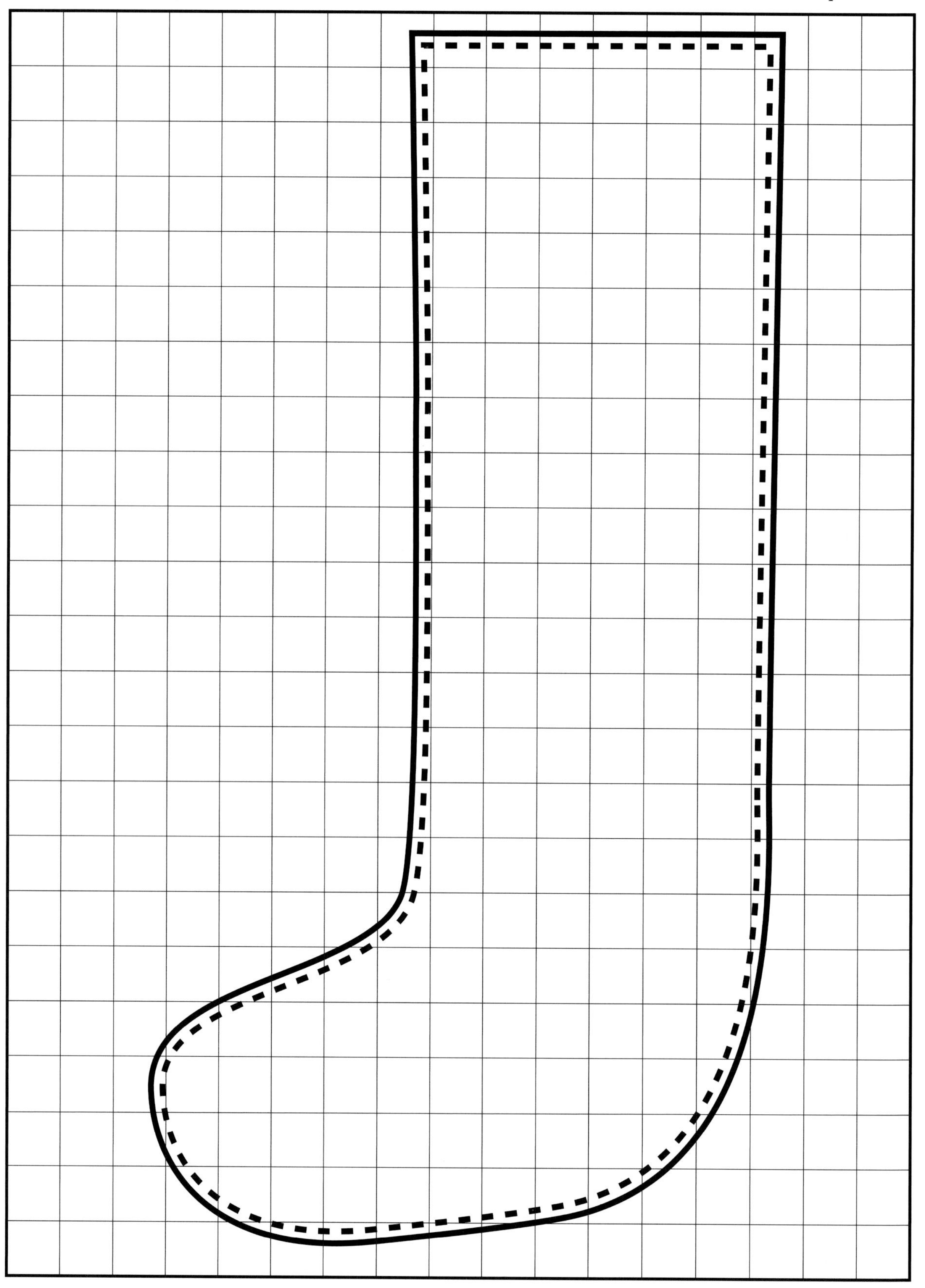

Bow-Trimmed Bootie

1 square = 1"

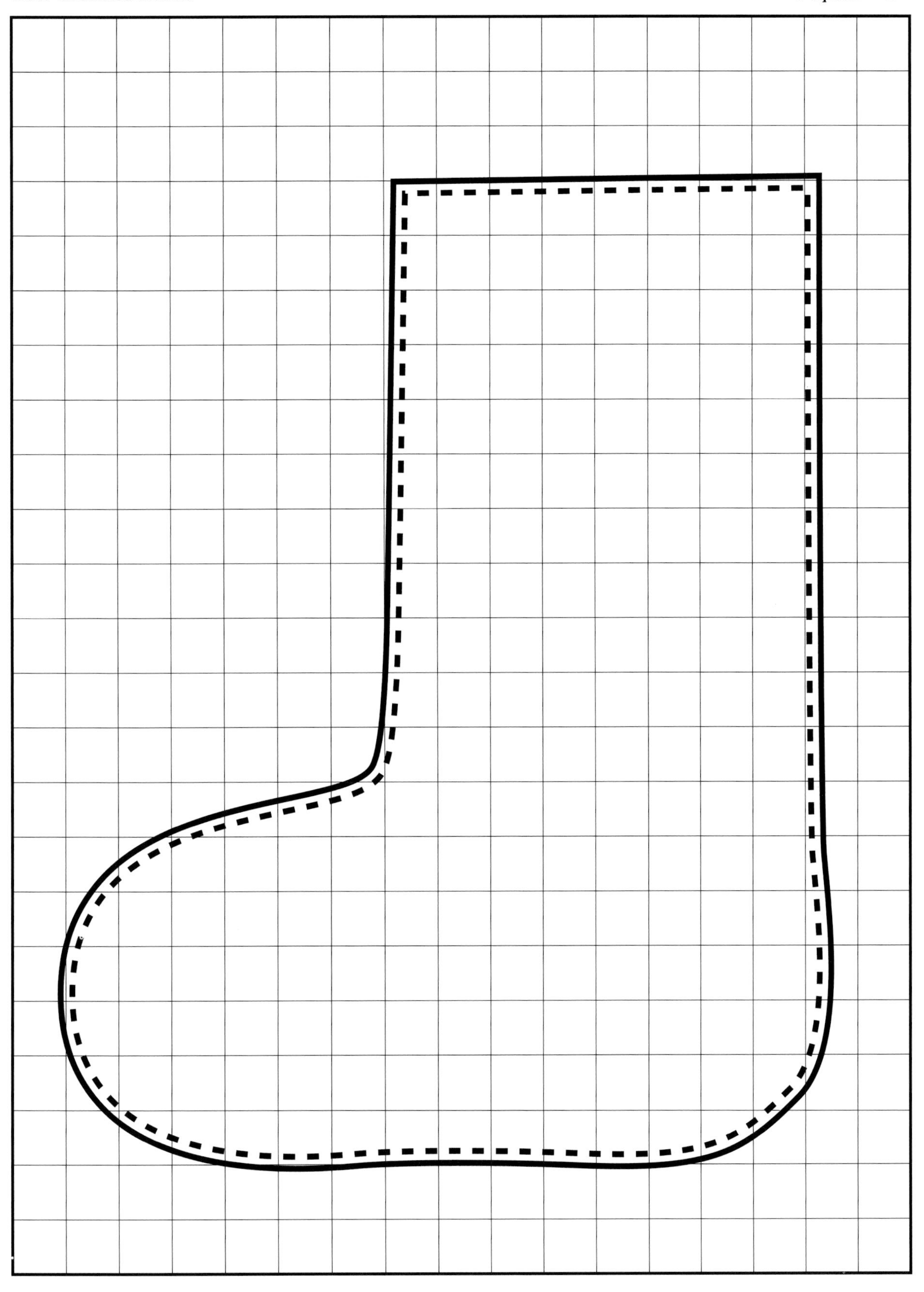

PATCHWORK STOCKING, POM-POM STOCKING

You need: 1/4 yd each of print fabric remnants; 1/2 yd of pom-pom trim; 1/4 yd of narrow cord; 16 wood beads in Christmas colors.
Cutting: Enlarge desired pattern (this page or page 127). From one print fabric, cut two stocking sections for front and back. For Patchwork, from second print fabric, cut three patch shapes. From another print fabric, cut one cuff (16" x 5 1/2" for Patchwork, 14" x 4 1/2" for Pom-Pom).
Sewing: (***Note:*** All stitching is done in 1/4" seams, with right sides facing and raw edges even, unless noted. Sew Pom-Pom Stocking same as Patchwork, ignoring how-to's on patches.) Pin patches to stocking front, raw edges even; baste along outer edges. Turn under 1/4" on remaining edges. Hand-stitch close to turned-under edges. Pin and stitch front to back along sides and lower edges, leaving upper edge open. Clip curves; turn right side out. Fold cuff in half crosswise; stitch short ends together. Slip cuff over upper edge of stocking. Pin and stitch one edge of cuff to upper edge of stocking, aligning seams. Turn under 1/4" on other edge of cuff; fold to inside of stocking, over cuff seam. Hand-stitch fold over seam. Fold cuff to right side of stocking. Pin trim under lower edge of cuff; stitch close to fold to attach trim.
Finishing: String beads onto cord; knot ends together to form hanging loop. Hand-stitch loop inside upper back corner of stocking.

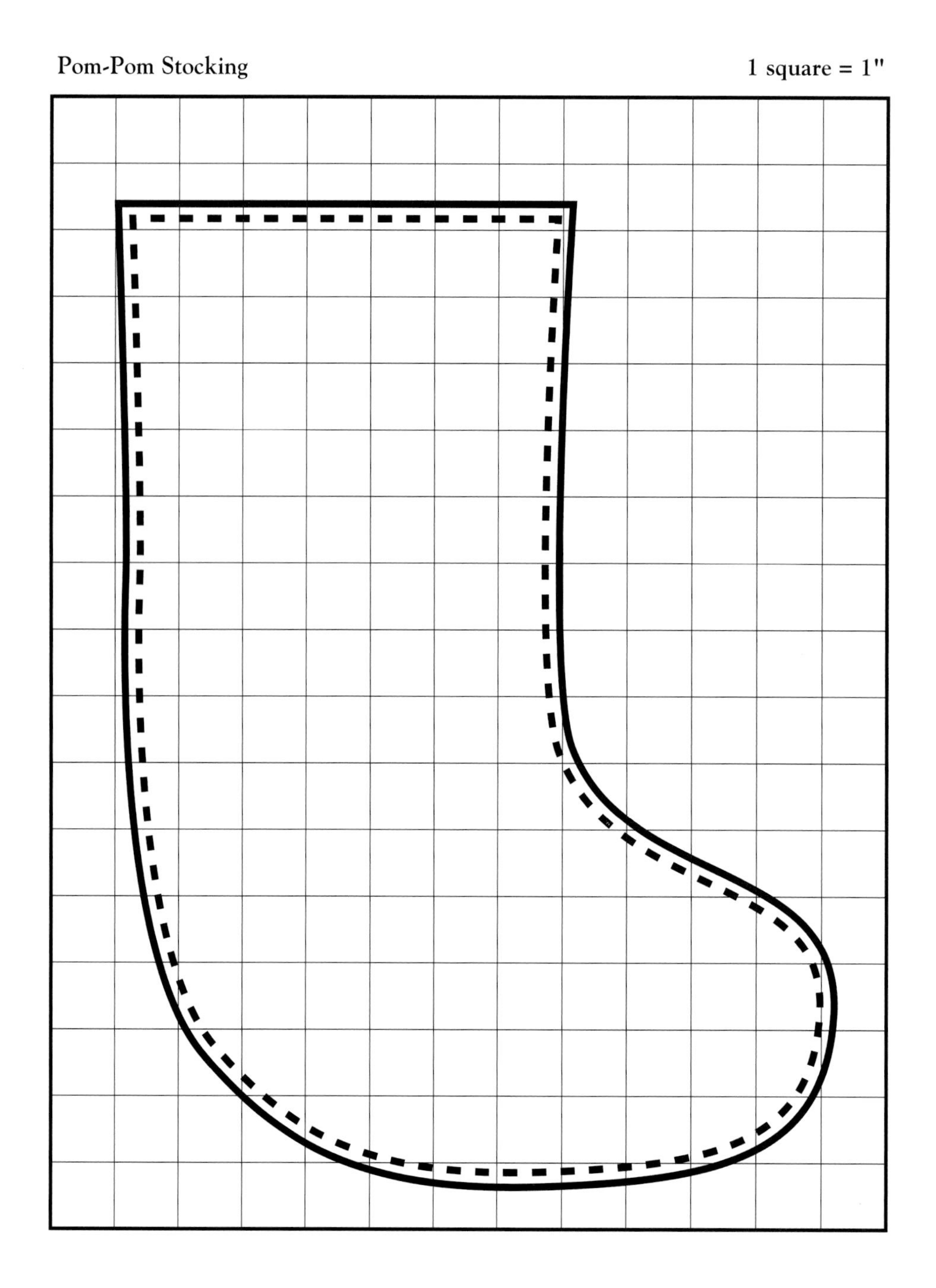

Patchwork Stocking 1 square = 1"

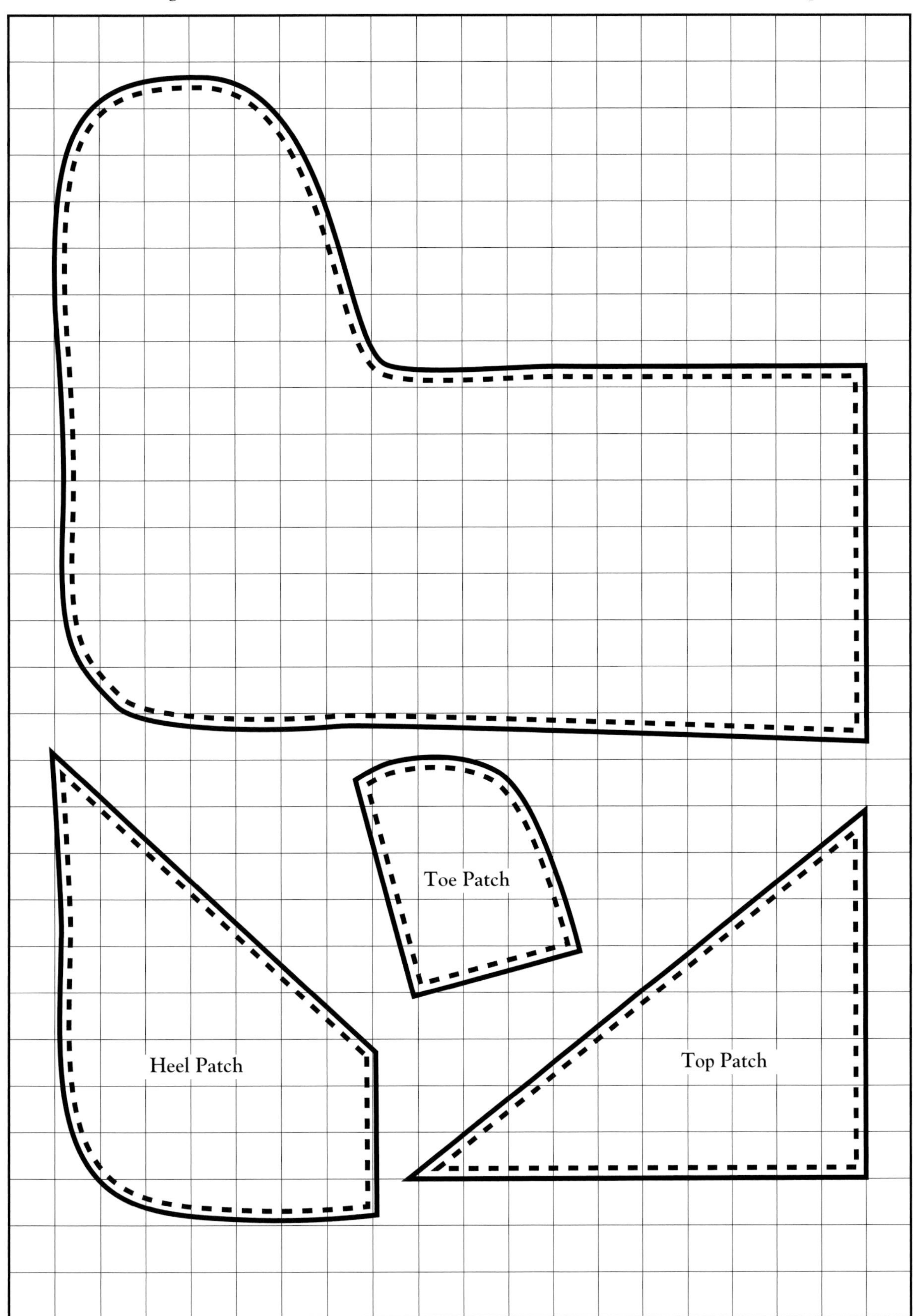

MERRY CANDLESTICKS

You need: Wood beads and disks; wood glue; candle cup; paintbrushes; acrylic paints – green, white, red; spray sealer.
Painting: Paint disk red. Paint beads, alternating red and green; let dry. Paint white checks on disk; let dry.
Finishing: Stack and glue beads on disk. Glue cup on top. Coat with sealer; let dry.

FROSTY SNOWMEN

You need: Wood snowman-shaped candle holders; sandpaper; paintbrushes; gesso; acrylic paints – off-white, soft black, green, orange, red; small wood ball; wood glue; remnants of green wool fabric or red-and-white string; small white buttons.
Painting: Sand candle holders; coat with gesso. Let dry. Paint hats and inside holes with black paint. Paint bodies off-white. Paint wood ball orange; glue to center of face for nose. Dip brush handle in black paint to make dots for eyes and mouth. Mix small amounts of red and off-white paints to make pink; apply lightly to cheeks. Paint tiny off-white dot in each eye. Paint small black eyebrows above eyes. Paint green wreath or red band with off-white dots around hat. Paint rim of candle hole off-white. Paint red or green checks on rim.
Finishing: For wool scarf, cut 3/8" x 5" strip of wool fabric for scarf; make tiny cuts on each end to form fringe. For string scarf, cut 5" of string. Tie around neck. Glue buttons to front of snowman.

SANTA AND SANTA'S HELPER APRONS

You need: Cotton fabrics – 1 yd red solid, 1 1/2 yds red/white checked or plaid, remnants of white, flesh, pink and brown; paper-backed fusible web; transfer paper; tapestry wool – light blue, bright green; sewing machine with buttonhole foot.
Cutting: (*Note:* Cutting sizes are given for adult size; measurements in parentheses are for child size.) From red solid fabric, cut two 11" (8") squares for bib and bib lining, two 4" x 31" (4" x 24") pieces for waistband and waistband lining, and two 8" x 10" (6" x 8") pieces for pockets. From checked or plain fabric, cut one 22" x 31" (18" x 24") skirt, two 2" x 81" (3" x 60") straps (piecing as needed), and one 3" x 11" (3" x 8") binding strip.
Decorating bibs: Enlarge patterns (page 129). Trace each section of each pattern onto paper side of web, leaving 1/2" between sections. Cut out sections roughly, leaving paper border around each. Following web manufacturer's directions, fuse web pieces onto wrong sides of fabric remnants; cut out along outlines. Arrange pieces on front of each bib; fuse appliqués to each bib. Set machine to wide zigzag stitch; sew around edges of each appliqué section with matching thread. Using transfer paper and pencil, transfer lettering to bib. Using tapestry wool and chain stitches, embroider lettering; using satin stitches, embroider eyes. Press.
Sewing: (*Note:* All stitching is done in 1/2" seams, with right sides facing and raw edges even, unless noted.) Place bib on bib lining, wrong sides facing. Baste edges; work with both layers together. Turn under 1/2" on each long edge of binding; press. Fold binding in half lengthwise, wrong sides facing and pressed edges even; press. Slip upper edge of bib between folds of binding; pin. Stitch binding to bib close to fold, through all layers. Turn under 1/4" on each long edge of each strap; press. Fold each strap in half lengthwise, wrong sides facing and pressed edges even; press. Slip sides of bib between folds of each strap, placing one end of each strap even with lower edge of bib. Stitch straps to bib close to folds, through all layers; continue to stitch long edges of each strap, stopping 1" from short ends. Turn under 1/2" on short end of each strap; finish sewing long edges, pivoting at corner to stitch across short ends. Pin lower (unfinished) edge of bib to center of one long edge of waistband. Pin waistband lining to waistband, over bib; stitch short ends and bib edge. Trim corners; turn waistband right side out. Turn under 1/4", then 1/4" again, on each short edge and one long edge of skirt; press. Stitch close to edges to hem sides and lower edge of skirt. Pin and stitch remaining edge of skirt to lower (unfinished) edge of waistband, keeping waistband lining free. Turn under 1/2", then 1", on one long edge of each pocket; stitch close to folds to hem pockets. Turn under 1/2" on remaining edges of pockets, folding in fullness at corners; press. Hold apron up to body to determine pocket placement; mark with pins. Adjust placement so pockets are even. Pin pockets to skirt at marks; stitch close to pressed edges of pockets, leaving upper edges open.
Finishing: Make a 1" buttonhole at each end of waistband. Cross straps and slip ends through buttonholes; tie in bow at back.

1 square = 1"

PATCHWORK ALBUM

You need: Scrapbook with wood or cardboard cover; spray-mount adhesive; glue gun; cotton fabrics – 1/2 yd red plaid, remnants of assorted red prints; small square of embroidered fabric; 4 small red buttons; 2 large white buttons; 3 yds of 1"W red ribbon.

Cutting: Remove screws from binding of scrapbook. From plaid, cut two pieces, each 2" larger all around than scrapbook covers.

Making covers: Spray wrong side of each plaid piece with adhesive; center a cover on each piece, right sides down. Wrap fabric edges to wrong side, folding in fullness at each corner. Hot-glue fabric edges to covers.

Making patchwork: (*Note:* All stitching is done in 1/4" seams, with right sides facing and raw edges even, unless noted.) Trim embroidered fabric edges, if needed, to make square. Cut remaining fabric remnants into strips; vary widths of strips from 1" to 2 1/2". Pin and stitch narrow strips to upper and lower edges of square; press strip ends even with square edges. Pin and stitch narrow strips to remaining edges of square; press and trim in same way. Continue adding strips to each edge of square, adding wider strips each time until patchwork is 1" larger than cover all around. Press; trim if needed to form squared edges on patchwork.

Assembling: Turn under 1" on one edge of patchwork. Spray wrong side of patchwork with adhesive. Place patchwork right side up on front cover so pressed edge is even with book spine. Wrap edges to inside of cover, folding in fullness at corners. Hot-glue edges to inside of cover.

Finishing: Sew red buttons along one edge of front cover. Cut two 18" lengths of ribbon for ties. Stitch white button to front of each cover, through one tie end, to attach ties to covers. Glue remaining ribbon to inside covers, concealing fabric edges; fold each corner of ribbon at 45-degree angle to form miters. Reassemble scrapbook; replace screws in binding.

CHRISTMAS QUILT

You need: Cotton print fabrics – 3 yds red ticking stripe, 1 1/2 yds each of 5 other red or green prints, 3 yds print (backing); queen-size quilt batting.

Cutting: From red ticking, cut one 49 1/2" x 63 1/2" center section and forty 4 7/8" squares. Cut each square in half diagonally to make 80 border triangles. From remaining print fabrics, cut one hundred sixty-eight 4 7/8" squares. Cut 48 of these in half diagonally to make 96 edging triangles; remaining squares are used as border squares.

Assembling quilt front: (*Note:* All stitching is done with right sides facing and 1/4" seam, unless otherwise noted.) Pin and stitch border squares and triangles in strips (see diagram), alternating colors and prints. Pin and stitch strips to form four border sections. Pin and stitch border sections together at ends to form border. Pin and stitch border to edges of center section; clip to corners.

Making edging: Pin pairs of edging triangles together; stitch along both short sides. Turn to make 48 edging triangles. Pin and stitch edging triangles to edges of border triangles, raw edges even.

Finishing: Measure quilt front, excluding edging; add 1/2" all around. Cut backing to this measurement, piecing if needed, for quilt back. Baste batting to wrong side of quilt back; trim batting even with fabric. Pin quilt front to quilt back; stitch around edges, leaving opening along one edge. Turn; slipstitch opening closed. Quilt center panel as desire; quilt borders near edges of each border triangle and square.

Christmas Quilt Diagram

victorian beauties
(pages 22-29)

BROCADE BOOT

You need: 1/2 yd brocade fabric; 1 1/2 yds of 3/4"w gold-edged velvet ribbon; assorted buttons; hand-sewing needle.
Cutting: Enlarge pattern (below). From fabric, cut two stocking sections for front and back.
Sewing: Pin front to back along sides and lower edges, with right sides facing and raw edges even. Stitch pinned edges in 1/4" seams, leaving upper edge open. Clip curves; turn. Turn under 1/4", then 1/4" again, on upper edge of stocking; stitch close to fold to hem stocking. Hand-stitch ribbon to upper edge of stocking. Pin and stitch two more rows of ribbon, evenly spaced, below first row.
Finishing: Cut 10" of ribbon; fold in half to form hanging loop. Hand-stitch loop inside upper back corner of stocking. Sew buttons to stocking as desired.

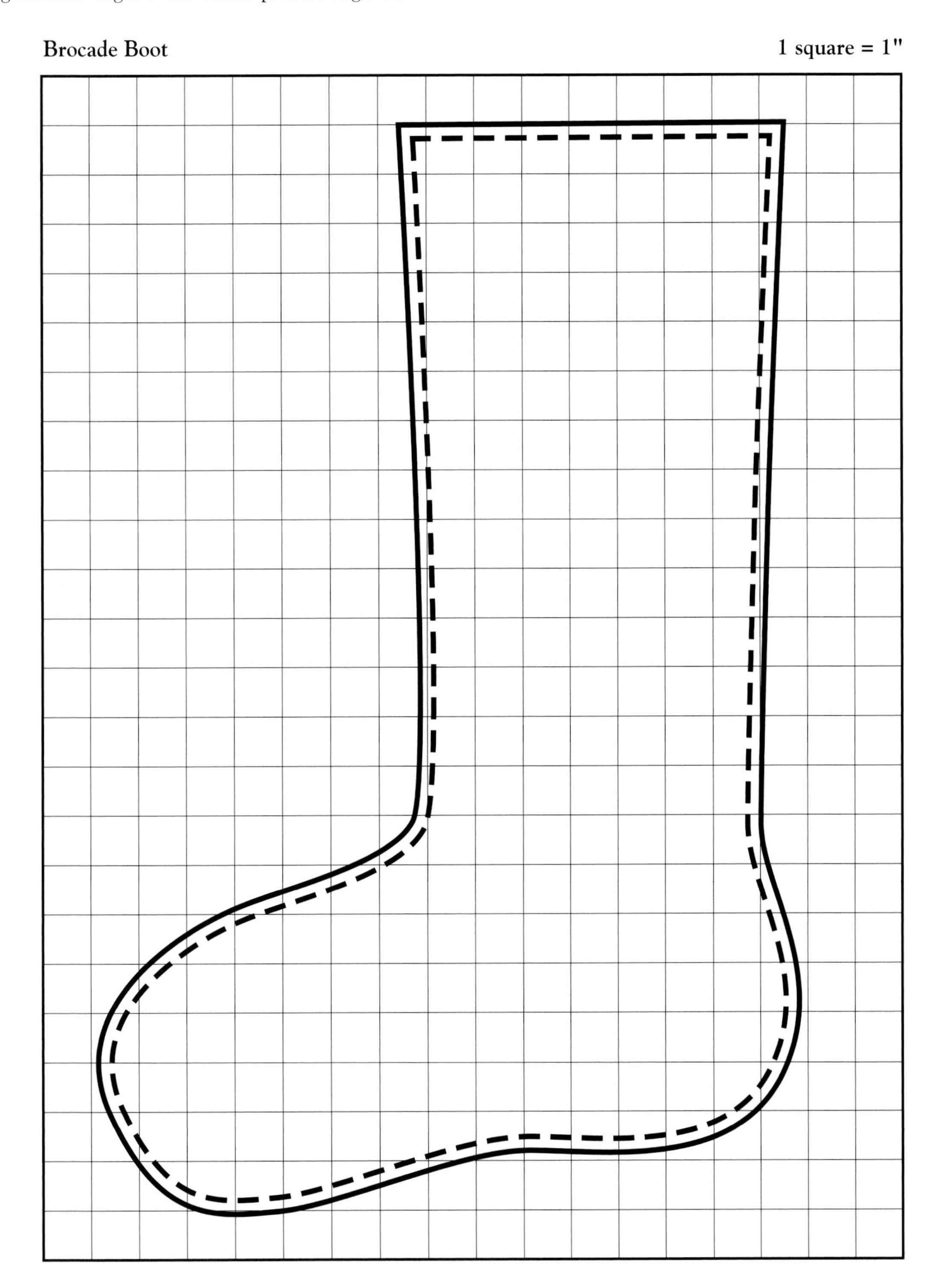

HIGH-BUTTON SHOE

You need: 1/2 yd brocade fabric; 1/4 yd contrasting velvet; 1"W cream ribbon; nine 1" buttons; hand-sewing needle.
Cutting: Enlarge pattern (below). From brocade, cut two stocking sections for front and back. From velvet, cut two cuff sections.
Sewing: (***Note:*** All stitching is done in 1/4" seams, with right sides facing and raw edges even, unless noted.) Pin and stitch a cuff to upper edge of front. Pin and stitch remaining cuff to upper edge of back. Pin and stitch front to back along sides and lower edges, leaving upper edge open. Clip curves; turn. Turn under 1/4", then 1/4" again, on upper edge of stocking; stitch close to fold to hem stocking.
Finishing: Cut 6" of ribbon; fold in half to form hanging loop. Hand-stitch loop inside upper back corner of stocking. Pin ribbon to front seam of stocking; turn under raw ends. Hand-stitch ribbon to stocking. Sew buttons to center of ribbon.

FRINGE BOOTIE

You need: 1/2 yd brocade fabric; 1/2 yd upholstery fringe; 1" button; hand-sewing needle.

Cutting: Enlarge pattern (below). From fabric, cut two stocking sections for front and back and one 3" x 8" hanging loop.

Sewing: Pin front to back along sides and lower edges, with right sides facing and raw edges even. Stitch pinned edges in 1/4" seams, leaving upper edge open. Clip curves; turn. Turn under 1/4", then 1/4" again, on upper edge of stocking; stitch close to fold to hem stocking. Pin fringe around upper edge of stocking; hand-stitch in place.

Finishing: Fold hanging loop in half lengthwise, right sides facing; stitch long edge in 1/4" seam. Turn; fold in half. Hand-stitch loop inside upper back corner of stocking. Sew button to cuff at base of hanging loop.

SILK AND PEARL STOCKING

You need: 3/4 yd pearl-embroidered silk fabric; paper; 1/2 yd tassel trim; 6" length of 1"W sheer ribbon.

Cutting: Draw or trace freehand leg shape on paper to make pattern. From fabric, cut two stocking sections for front and back.

Sewing: Pin front to back along sides and lower edges, with right sides facing and raw edges even. Stitch pinned edges in 1/4" seams, leaving upper edge open. Clip curves; turn. Turn under 1/4", then 1/4" again, on upper edge of stocking; stitch close to fold to hem stocking. Pin trim around upper edge of stocking; hand-stitch in place.

Finishing: Fold ribbon in half to form hanging loop. Hand-stitch loop inside upper back corner of stocking.

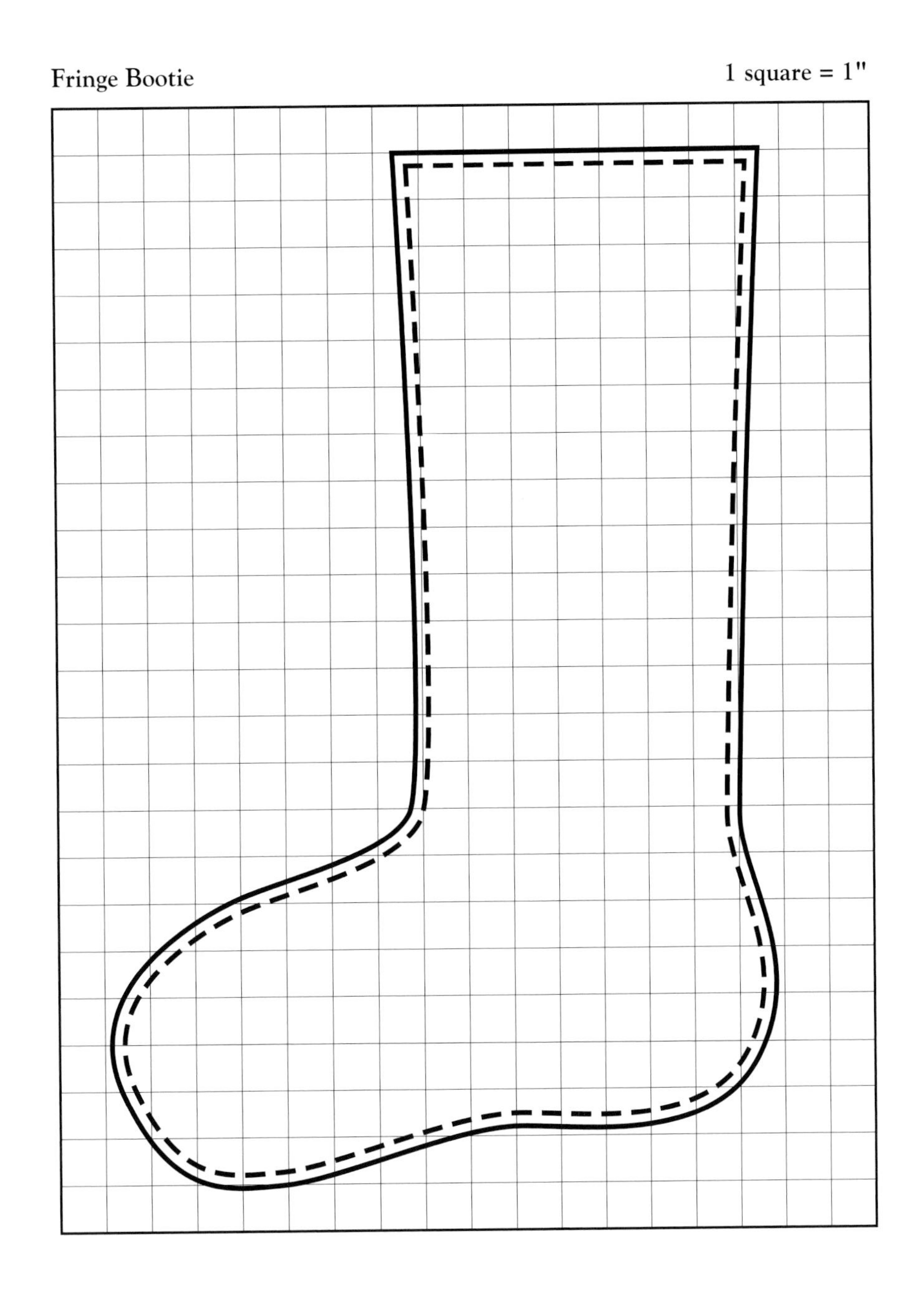

BROCADE DOVES (continued)

Sewing: (***Note:*** All stitching is done in 1/4" seams, with right sides facing and raw edges even, unless noted.) Pin and stitch body sections together, leaving open between marks. Pin and stitch one side of gusset to one body section, matching marks. Clip corners; trim seams, Turn; stuff. Slipstitch remaining side closed. Pin and stitch tail pieces together, leaving short straight end open; turn. Turn under raw edge of tail; pin tail to dove, about 1/2" from back point, centering tail on top of dove. Slipstitch tail to body.

RIBBON ROSETTES

You need (for each): 1 yd of 1"W velvet ribbon; glue gun; 1/4 yd of 1"W embroidered ribbon; 1/4 yd of 1/2"W satin ribbon; small pearl; 1/4 yd of narrow ribbon or cord.
Assembling: Cut velvet ribbon into four equal pieces for loops. Overlap and glue ends of each piece 1". Overlap loops and stitch through center. Fold embroidered ribbon in half crosswise; stitch short ends together to form ring. Sew running stitches along one edge of ring; pull up threads to gather into flower. Sew to center of rosette. Form flower from satin ribbon in same way; sew in center of other flower. Glue pearl in center. Fold narrow ribbon in half to form hanging loop; sew ends to back of rosette.

VICTORIAN TREE SKIRT

You need: 2 yds champagne jacquard fabric; chalk pencil; assorted ribbons.
Cutting: Fold fabric in quarters. Starting at fold point, mark curved lines 4" and 28" from center. Cut along lines through all layers. Slash from outer edge to inner circle.
Assembling: Turn under 1/4", then 1/4" again, on cut edges; press. Stitch close to folds to hem skirt. Hand-stitch ribbon from center to edge in several places. Tie additional ribbon in bows; hand-sew to skirt.

DOORKNOB POSY

You need: slender vase; decorative paper; tape; gold cord; floral braid; fresh roses and berries.
To do: Wrap vase with paper; tape in place. Wind cord and braid around vase as desired, knotting to secure and making sure to leave a loop of cord for hanger. Tuck berries and roses in vase.

VELVET PET PILLOW

You need: 1 3/4 yds green velvet; 1 3/4 yds cotton underlining; 3 1/2 yds of pale gold twisted-satin cording; 4 large tan tassels; fiberfill stuffing.
Cutting: Cut two 25" squares each of velvet and underlining. Pin underlining to wrong side of velvet for pillow top and bottom.
Sewing: (***Note:*** All stitching is done in 1" seams, with right sides facing and raw edges even, unless noted.) Pin and stitch cording to right side of top, with cording 1" from fabric edges. Pin and hand-stitch tassels to right side of top at corners, tassels toward center. Pin and stitch top to bottom, leaving opening on one side; turn. Stuff; slipstitch opening closed.

TREAT SACK

You need: 1/2 yd champagne-colored fabric with pearl embroidery; 1/2 yd green velvet fabric; teacup; chalk pencil; 3 yds of 1/2"w ribbon; safety pin.
Cutting: From each fabric, cut two 11" x 9" pieces for bag (pearl fabric) and lining (velvet). Trace teacup at two lower corners of one bag section; cut along marked lines to form shaped lower edge. Using cut piece as pattern, cut each remaining piece in same way.
Sewing: (***Note:*** All stitching is done in 1/4" seams, with right sides facing and raw edges even, unless noted.) Pin and stitch a bag section to each lining section along upper edge. Pin these joined pieces together along outer edges, with seams aligned. Stitch edges, leaving a 3/4" opening on each side of bag 1 1/2" from seam. Also leave 3" opening in lining for turning. Clip curves; turn. Slipstitch lining opening closed. Push lining into bag. For casing, stitch 1 1/2" and 2 1/2" from upper edge. Cut ribbon in half. Tie end of one ribbon to safety pin. Insert ribbon into one side opening and through casing, pulling ribbon out through same opening. Knot ends together. Insert remaining ribbon through other opening in same way.

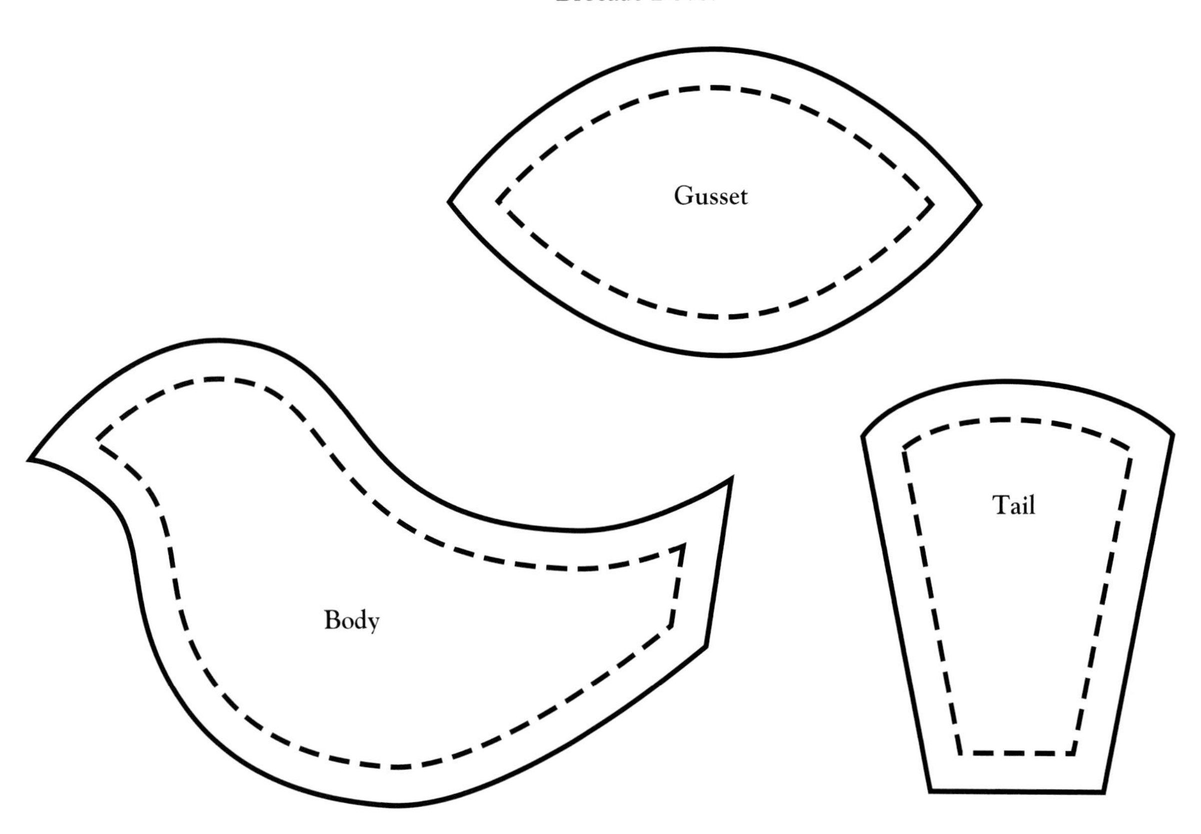

naturally christmas

(pages 30-37)

PINECONE GLOBE

You need: 6" plastic foam ball; brown spray paint; wire cutters; pinecones; low-temp glue gun.
To do: Spray foam ball with brown paint. Use wire cutters to cut off bottoms of cones. Glue bottoms of cones to ball. Fill in areas with remaining parts of cones.

PINECONE GARLAND

You need: Heavy nylon fishing line; small and large pinecones; small gold ball ornaments.
To do: Thread large pinecone, small pinecone, large pinecone, and two ball ornaments onto line, repeating sequence to desired length. (Secure pinecones by wrapping line once around center of pinecone.)

GILDED TERRA-COTTA POTS

You need (for each): Small terra-cotta pot; gilding kit; paintbrushes; masking tape; acrylic jewels; glue gun.
Preparing pot: Wipe pots with damp cloth to remove any dust; let dry. Cover hole in bottom of pot with masking tape (inside and outside.)
Decorating pot: Follow gilding kit instructions to gild outside and inside of pot. Glue jewels to rim of pot.

CHRISTMAS PLAID AWNING

You need: Kraft paper or butcher paper (for pattern); plaid fabric; 5 tassels.
Making pattern: Measure width of furniture piece; add 1". Measure depth of furniture piece; add 18". Cut a piece of paper this size. Fold paper widthwise into five equal sections. Mark a 16"H triangle at one short edge of folded paper (point of triangle at center of paper's edge). Cut out triangle. Unfold paper.
Making awning: Using pattern, cut two fabric pieces, piecing if needed. Using a 1/2" seam allowance, sew pieces together, leaving an opening on long edge. Turn right side out; press.
Finishing: Sew tassels to points of awning.

twinkle, twinkle
(pages 38-43)

SILVERY BEAD ORNAMENTS

You need (for each ornament): 22-gauge spool wire; wire cutters; needle-nose pliers; beads – 4 dozen small crystal rocaille, 2 dozen larger gray/silver round; 2 dozen crystal bugle beads; 8" of sheer ribbon in desired color.
Assembling: For ornament shown on page 38, cut four 5" pieces of wire. Using pliers, bend one end of one wire into tiny loop to prevent beads from slipping off. Thread a small, then a large bead onto wire. Thread on beads, alternating as desired, until wire is half-covered. Hold remaining wires together at midpoints. Twist center of beaded wire around midpoints of remaining wires. Arrange wire ends to form star shape. Finish threading beads on other end of beaded wire in same way; bend end into loop. Thread beads on each end of each remaining wire in same way, bending each end into loop when beads are threaded. (See photos, pages 39 and 41, for more designs.)
Finishing: Slip ribbon through one loop. Knot ribbon ends together to form hanging loop.

STAR-STAMPED WRAPS

You need: Foam brushes; star-shaped stencil; fabric paints – white, silver, medium blue; star-shaped rubber stamp; large sheets of paper – white, deep blue, silver; fine-point paint pens – blue, silver; small sea sponge; white translucent craft paint; organza or chiffon fabrics – blue, white; assorted ribbons; plastic clothes hanger.
Decorating paper: Brush silver or blue fabric paint onto star stamp; stamp on white paper and let dry. Using paint pens, write Christmas-carol lyrics on white paper; let dry. Dip sponge in translucent paint; sponge randomly on silver paper and let dry.
Decorating fabric: Place fabric on white paper. Place stencil on fabric. Using foam brush, dab contrasting fabric paint through stencil onto fabric. When paint dries, both fabric and paper may be used to wrap packages.
Painting ribbon: Drape ribbon over hanger. Using foam brush, paint ribbon with fabric paint, allowing ribbon color to show through in spots.
Wrapping: Wrap packages as desired with decorated papers and fabrics. Wrap some packages with silver or blue paper first, then wrap again with fabric. Tie ribbon around packages.

BAUBLE STAR DOOR DECORATION

You need: 22" square of 1"-thick plastic foam; permanent marker; serrated knife; about 40 small silver painted pinecones; about 60 shiny silver and 10 matte silver glass ball ornaments, 1" to 2" across; glue gun; about 60 pearl-head straight pins.
Cutting star: On a copier, enlarge star pattern (page 137) to 21"W; cut out. Trace pattern onto foam with marker. Cut out star with knife.
Preparing materials: Remove hooks and caps from ornaments; discard hooks.
Making star: Glue pinecones, wide sides down, to star; space cones evenly over foam. Glue ornaments, cap ends down, to fill spaces between cones. Bend sides of ornament caps out to make flowers. Insert pin through center of each flower, then into star, so no foam is visible.

Bauble Star Pattern

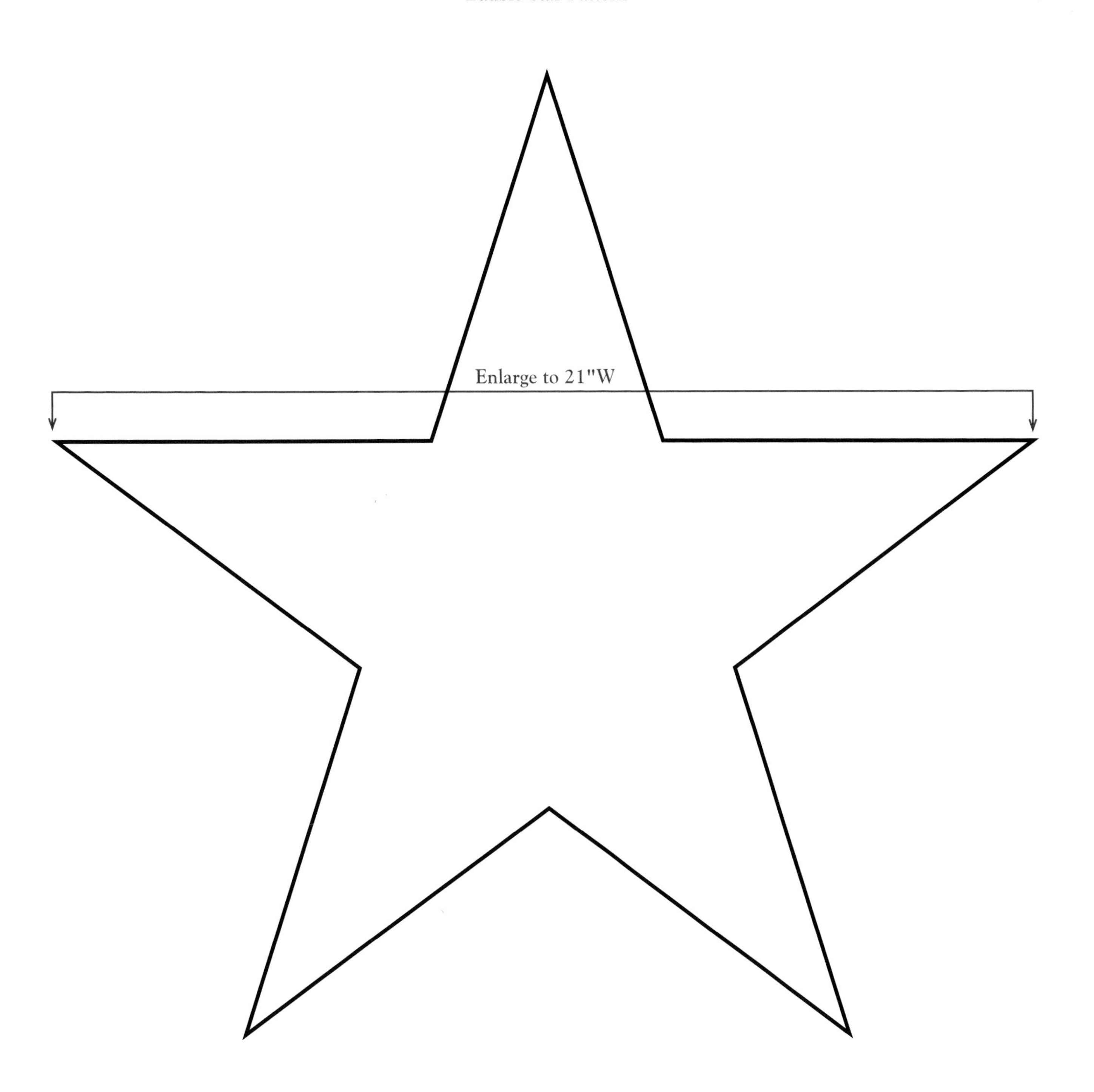

PAINTED CHRISTMAS BALLS

You need: Paintbrushes – 1" wash, small round; glossy water-based craft paints – silver, dark blue, light blue, white; wooden balls in assorted sizes; dark-blue translucent craft paint.
Painting: Using wash brush, coat each ball with glossy paint in desired base-coat color; let dry. For dotted ball, paint white dots on ball with round brush; let dry. Apply translucent paint over dots. For shimmering ball, paint silver stars on ball with round brush; let dry. Thin silver paint with water to make glaze; brush glaze onto ball. Let dry.

CELESTIAL ORNAMENTS

You need: Fabric remnants – velvet, organdy, silk; fiberfill stuffing; nylon thread; sequins and crystal beads; embroidery floss.
Cutting: Use full-sized patterns (pages 138-141) and cut two matching sections for each ornament from desired fabrics. For ball, cut eight matching sections. If desired, cut an organdy overlay of each pattern piece for a shimmery look; baste the two fabric layers together at edges. Pin sections together with right sides facing and raw edges even. Stitch in 1/4" seams, leaving opening along one edge. Turn; stuff. Slipstitch opening closed.
Embellishing: Using nylon thread, stitch sequins and beads to ornaments.
Finishing: Cut 12" of floss for each ornament. Stitch through top of ornament; tie floss ends together to make hanging loop.

Celestial Ornament
Crescent

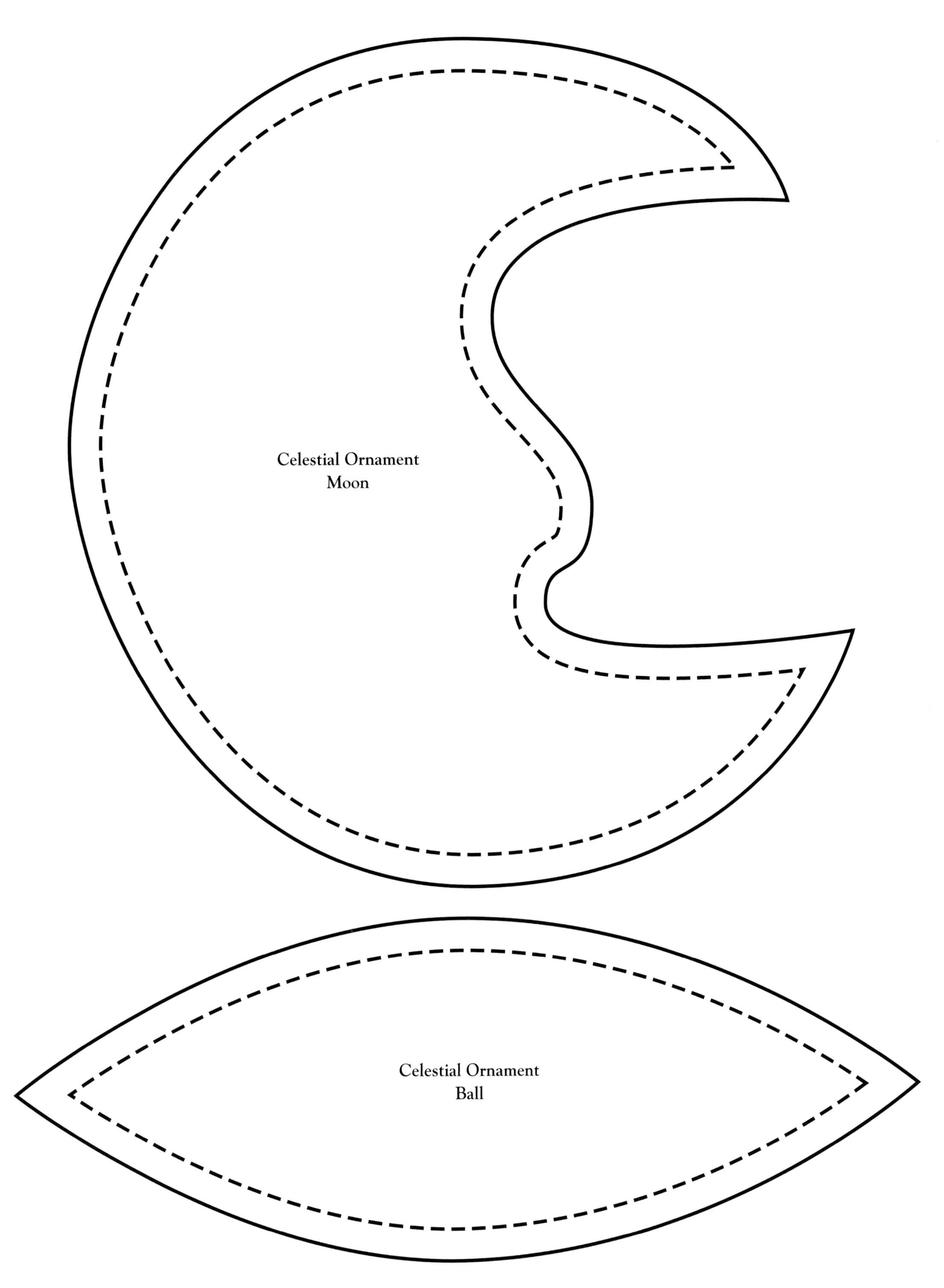
Celestial Ornament
Moon
Celestial Ornament
Ball

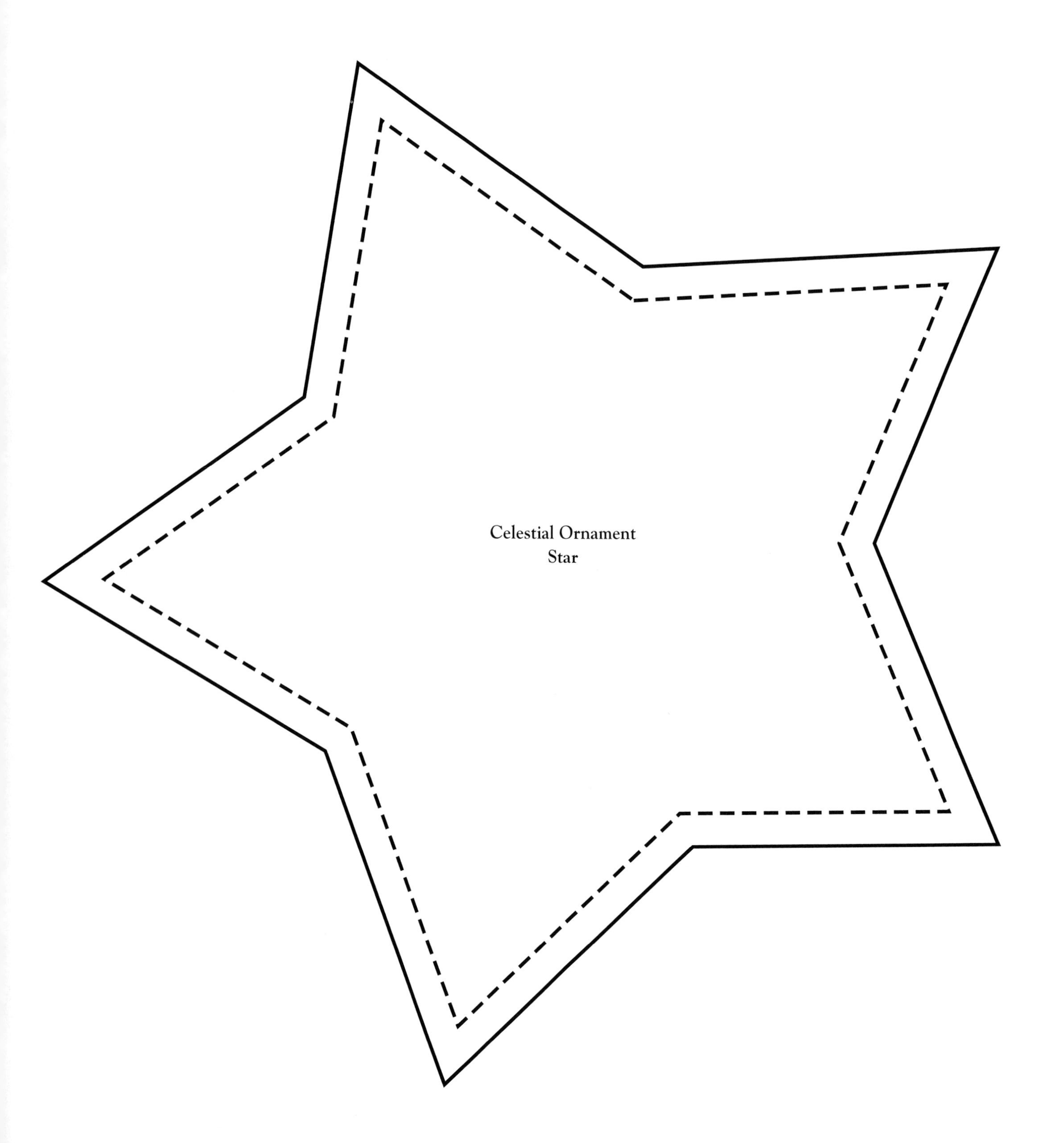
Celestial Ornament
Star

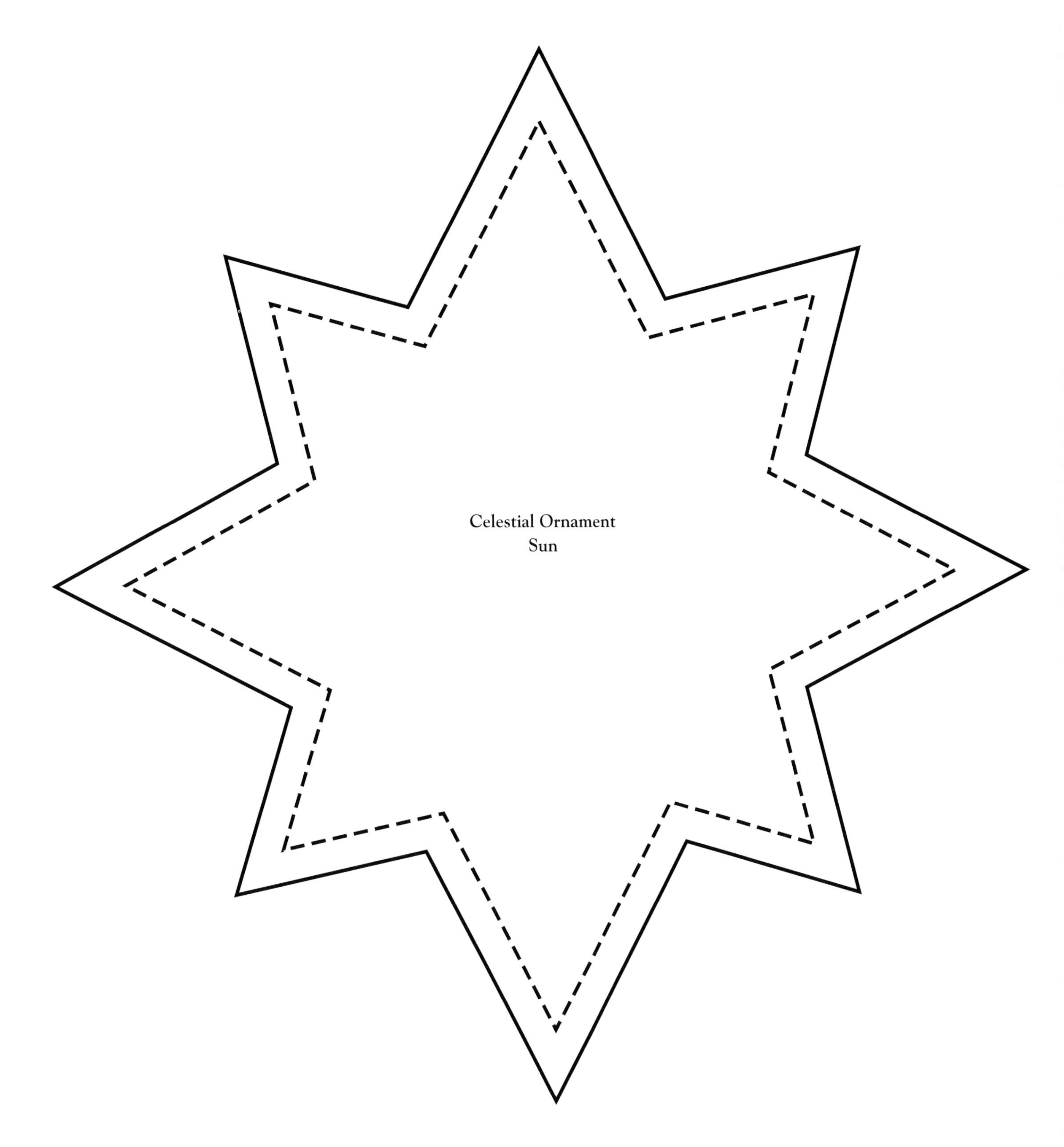
Celestial Ornament
Sun

FROSTED GINGERBREAD CASTLE

You need: Lightweight cardboard; rolling pin; 1 recipe Gingerbread Dough (page 77); craft knife; baking sheet; pastry bag with assorted tips; 3 recipes Royal Icing (page 77); assorted candies – white- and silver-coated candy ovals, silver dragées in assorted sizes (see Note below), 8 foil-wrapped chocolate candies; small sugared-cereal squares.
Making gingerbread pieces: Enlarge patterns (page 143); cut from cardboard. Roll out dough to 1/4" thick. Place patterns on dough; cut around pattern edges with crafts knife. Remove excess dough around pieces. Cut out windows; remove dough from inside windows. Cut out door. Cut heart in door; remove dough from inside heart. Use heart cutout as pattern to cut two hearts from remaining dough. Transfer pieces, including door, to baking sheet; bake according to recipe. Let cool.
Assembling base: Fit pastry bag with fine tip; fill with icing. Place front, back, and two side cottage sections on end; pipe icing where pieces meet to form cottage base.
Attaching roof: Place one roof section on cottage; pipe icing along side edges to attach. Place remaining roof section on cottage; pipe icing along side edges and at roof peak.
Decorating: *Pipe white icing where candies are to be adhered, unless otherwise noted; refer to photo for candy placement.* Press candy firmly into icing. Use wide piping tip to pipe frosting at corners of base. Pipe large amount of icing to center of one side of house for chimney "cement"; press white-coated candy and silver dragées into cement. Pipe icing on each side of chimney; press heart cookie into icing on each side. Adhere silver-coated candies along lower edges of house. Pipe icing around each window. Pipe icing onto roof; press wheat squares into icing for shingles. Pipe icing onto each shingle; press dragée into icing on each shingle. Pipe icing on roof at top of chimney; press white-coated candy into icing. Make chimney to desired height by adding layers of icing and candy. Pipe icing and attach remaining candies as desired (see photo, page 42).
Finishing: Pipe icing motifs on door, as pictured.
Note: Dragées are not recognized by the Food and Drug Administration as edible. Use for decoration only; remove before eating cookies.

SILVER CRACKERS

You need (for each): 12" x 8" sheet of silver kraft paper (if not available, coat brown kraft paper with silver spray paint); pinking shears; 4"L x 2" dia. paper tube; glue stick; 3/4 yd of 3/4"W silver ribbon; cracker snapper (from craft store); small toy, trinket or wrapped candy; craft glue; silver flower sequin.
Making cracker: From kraft paper, cut one 12" x 6" cracker cover and one 1 1/2" x 12" flower strip. Trim short ends of cover with pinking shears. Wrap cover lengthwise around paper tube so pinked ends extend evenly at tube ends. Using glue stick, glue paper to tube. Cut ribbon in two equal pieces; tie one ribbon in bow around paper at one end of tube. Insert cracker snapper and candy or trinket into tube; tie remaining ribbon in bow at open end of tube.
Embellishing: Fold flower strip crosswise, accordion-style, making pleats about 1/4" deep. Using glue stick, glue short ends of paper together to form flower. Glue pleat edges together at center of flower. Using craft glue, glue flower to cracker; glue sequin to center of flower.

1 square = 1"

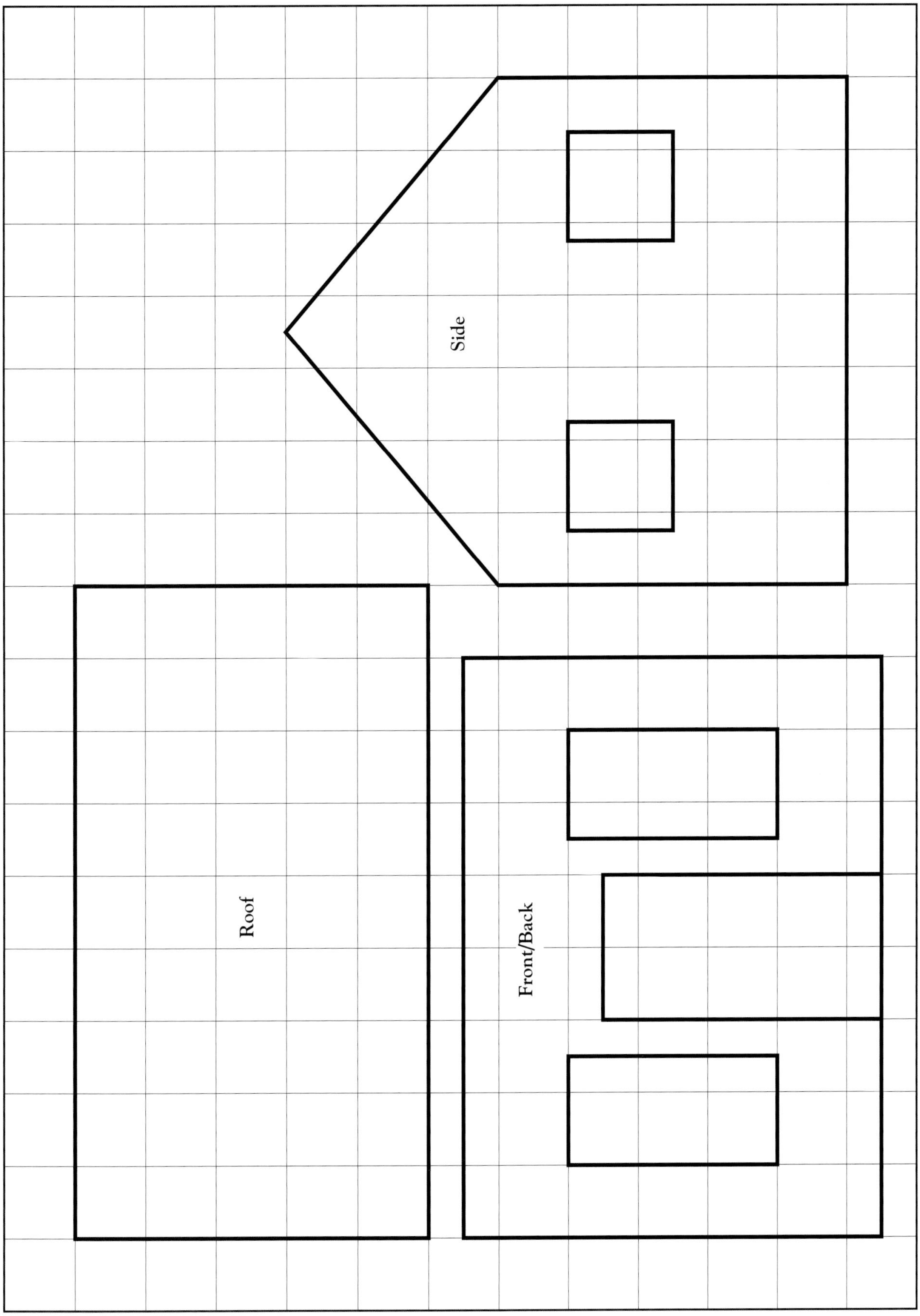

Side

Roof

Front/Back

sugar and spice (pages 44-51)

BUTLER CLAUS

You need: Transfer paper; 2' x 4' of 1/2" birch plywood; 3 1/2' of 1/2" x 2" lattice strip; 3' of molding; C-clamps; handheld electric jigsaw; 8 1/2" x 11 1/2" of 1/4" plywood; sandpaper; 3/16" drill; wood glue; 1/2" brads; paintbrushes; wood-primer spray; enamel paints – green, black, white, pink, blue, red, yellow; 10" x 22" of 1" pine; 2" wood star; 16' of white "rope" molding; 2 washers; 2 nuts; three 3/16" stove bolts with cap nuts, 1 1/4"L; ten 3/4" flathead wood screws; clear acrylic spray sealer.

Cutting: Enlarge pattern (this page). On birch plywood, mark one body, one nose, two arms, and four foot pieces. On lattice strip, mark two 9" and two 12" lengths for tray. On molding, mark one 8" hatband, two 3" sleeve cuffs, and two 5" pants cuffs. Clamp wood onto work surface; cut out; sand edges. Drill three holes in center of one 12" tray strip.

Assembling tray: Glue lattice strips together at corners to form 12" x 9" frame; secure glued corners with brads. Glue 1/4" plywood to bottom of frame to form tray.

Painting: Coat all wood pieces with primer. Paint pine base and tray green. Paint feet black. Paint hatband, sleeve cuffs, and pants cuffs white. Paint black and white stripes on legs. Paint face pink. Paint blue mittens on arms. Paint nose, rest of body, and rest of arms red. Paint star yellow.

Assembling: Glue lengths of rope molding to face for beard. Glue washers and nuts to face for eyes. Glue nose below eyes. Paint red mouth. Glue hatband and cuffs in place. Use stove bolts to attach tray to body. Use wood screws to attach lower arms to sides of tray, and upper arms to sides of body. Glue one foot piece to each side of each of Santa's ankles, keeping lower edges even. Use wood screws to attach base to feet. Glue star to tip of hat. Spray entire project with several light coats of sealer; let dry.

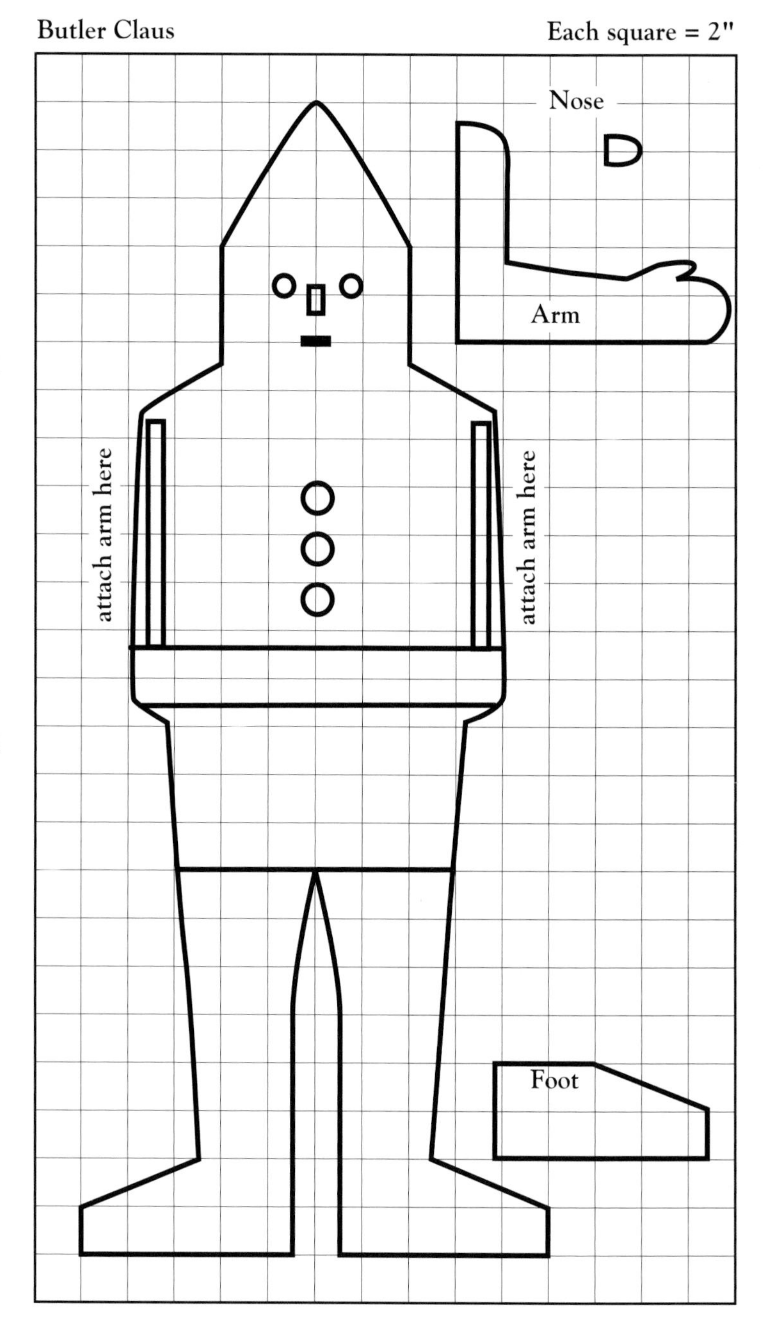

PLAID STOCKING

You need: Fabric – 5/8 yd plaid taffeta, 3/8 yd light green textured; 3/8 yd of multicolored ball fringe.
Cutting fabric: Enlarge stocking pattern (right); add 1/4" seam allowances; cut out. From plaid fabric, cut two stocking pieces (one in reverse) and one 2" x 8" loop. From light green, cut one 12" x 13 1/2" cuff.
Stitching: *Stocking* – Pin stocking pieces together, right sides facing; stitch 1/4" seam. Clip curves; turn right side out. *Loop* – Press under 8"L edges 1/4". Fold in half lengthwise (3/4" x 8"); topstitch. *Cuff* – Fold piece in half lengthwise with wrong sides together. Fold in half widthwise; stitch across short raw edge. Turn right side out.
Assembling: Slip loop inside stocking (at back edge), loop facing downward, raw edges even; baste. Slip cuff inside stocking (right side of cuff facing inside of stocking), raw edges even. Stitch around top edge. Pull out cuff; turn down.
Finishing: Pin and stitch ball fringe around bottom edge of cuff.

POCKET STOCKING

You need: Fabric – 5/8 yd textured green; 3/8 yd plaid taffeta.
Cutting fabric: Enlarge stocking pattern (right); add 1/4" seam allowances; cut out. From green fabric, cut two stocking pieces (one in reverse) and one 2" x 8" loop. From plaid, cut one 12 1/2" x 13 1/2" cuff and one 8 1/2" x 3 3/4" pocket.
Making pocket: Press under all edges 1/4". Fold piece in half to 4" x 3 1/4" (folded edge is top of pocket). Pin to front stocking piece with top of pocket 7" from stocking top. Topstitch pocket sides and bottom.
Stitching: *Stocking* – Pin stocking pieces together, right sides facing; stitch 1/4" seam. Clip curves; turn right side out. *Loop* – Press under 8"L edges 1/4". Fold in half lengthwise (3/4" x 8"); topstitch. *Cuff* – Fold piece in half lengthwise with wrong sides together. Fold in half widthwise; stitch across short raw edge. Turn right side out.
Assembling: Slip loop inside stocking (at back edge), loop facing downward, raw edges even; baste. Slip cuff inside stocking (right side of cuff facing inside of stocking), raw edges even. Stitch around top edge. Pull out cuff; turn down.

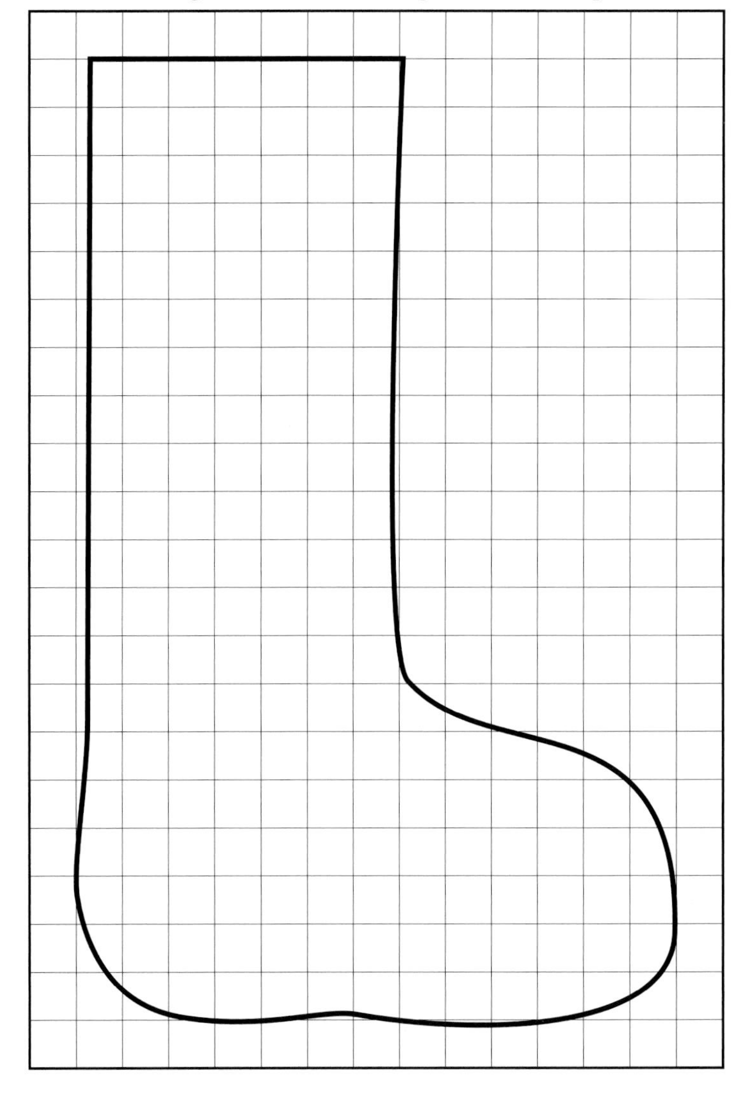

JESTER STOCKING

You need: Fabric – 5/8 yd red, 1/4 yd red/white ticking; 14" of yellow/white 2 1/2"W tasseled fringe; 1 1/4" jingle bell.

Cutting fabric: Enlarge stocking pattern (below); add 1/4" seam allowances all around; cut out. From red fabric, cut two stocking pieces (one in reverse). From red/white ticking, cut one 10 1/2" x 13" cuff and one 2" x 6" loop.

Stitching: *Stocking* – Pin stocking pieces together, right sides facing; stitch 1/4" seam. Clip curves; turn right side out. *Loop* – Press under 6"L edges 1/4". Fold in half lengthwise (3/4" x 6"); topstitch. *Cuff* – Fold piece in half lengthwise with wrong sides together. Fold in half widthwise; stitch across short raw edge. Turn right side out.

Assembling: Slip loop inside stocking (at back edge), loop facing downward, raw edges even; baste. Slip cuff inside stocking, right side facing inside of stocking, raw edges even. Stitch around top edge. Pull out cuff; turn down.

Finishing: Pin and stitch tasseled fringe around bottom edge of cuff. Sew bell to tip of toe.

CANDY CANE STOCKING

You need: 2/3 yd red-white ticking fabric; 14" of green 7"W bullion fringe.

Cutting fabric: Enlarge pattern (page 147); add 1/4" seam allowances; cut out. Cut two stocking pieces (one in reverse). Cut one 10 1/2" x 13" cuff and one 2" x 6" loop.

Stitching: *Stocking* – Pin stocking pieces together, right sides facing; stitch 1/4" seam. Clip curves; turn right side out. *Loop* – Press under 6"L edges 1/4". Fold in half lengthwise (3/4" x 6"); topstitch. *Cuff* – Fold piece in half lengthwise with wrong sides together. Fold in half widthwise; stitch across short raw edge. Turn right side out.

Assembling: Slip loop inside stocking (at back edge), loop facing downward, raw edges even; baste. Slip cuff inside stocking, right side facing inside of stocking, raw edges even. Stitch around top edge. Pull out cuff; turn down.

Finishing: Pin and stitch bullion fringe around bottom edge of cuff.

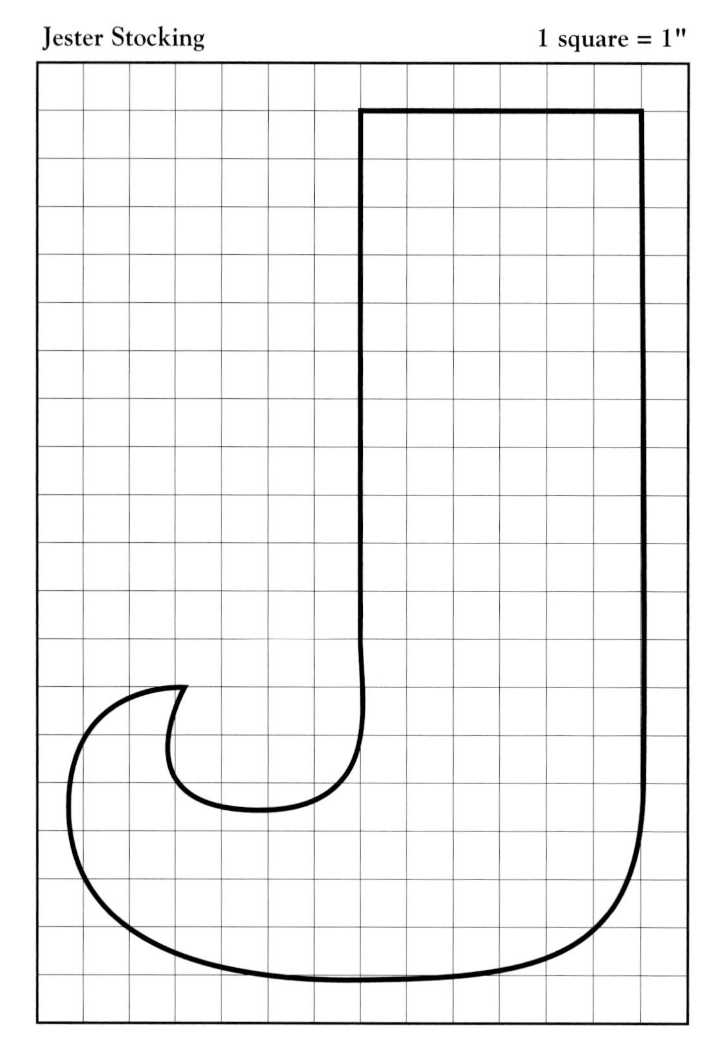

CINNAMON STICK BUNDLES

You need: 8"L cinnamon sticks; 1½"W ribbon; floral wire.
To do: Gather seven cinnamon sticks; wrap bundle with ribbon; tie ends in bow. Thread wire through ribbon at back; twist ends together to form loop for hanger.

FRUIT POMANDERS

You need: Fresh fruit (oranges, lemons, limes); whole cloves; 1"W sheer ribbon.
To do: Push stems of cloves into fruit, working around fruit to form a pattern. Wrap with ribbon; tie bow.

LACE GARLAND

You need: 1⅞"W Battenberg lace (by the yard); paintbrush; pearl white acrylic paint; white iridescent glitter.
To do: Paint lace; while wet, dip points in glitter; let dry.

Candy Cane Stocking

1 square = 1"

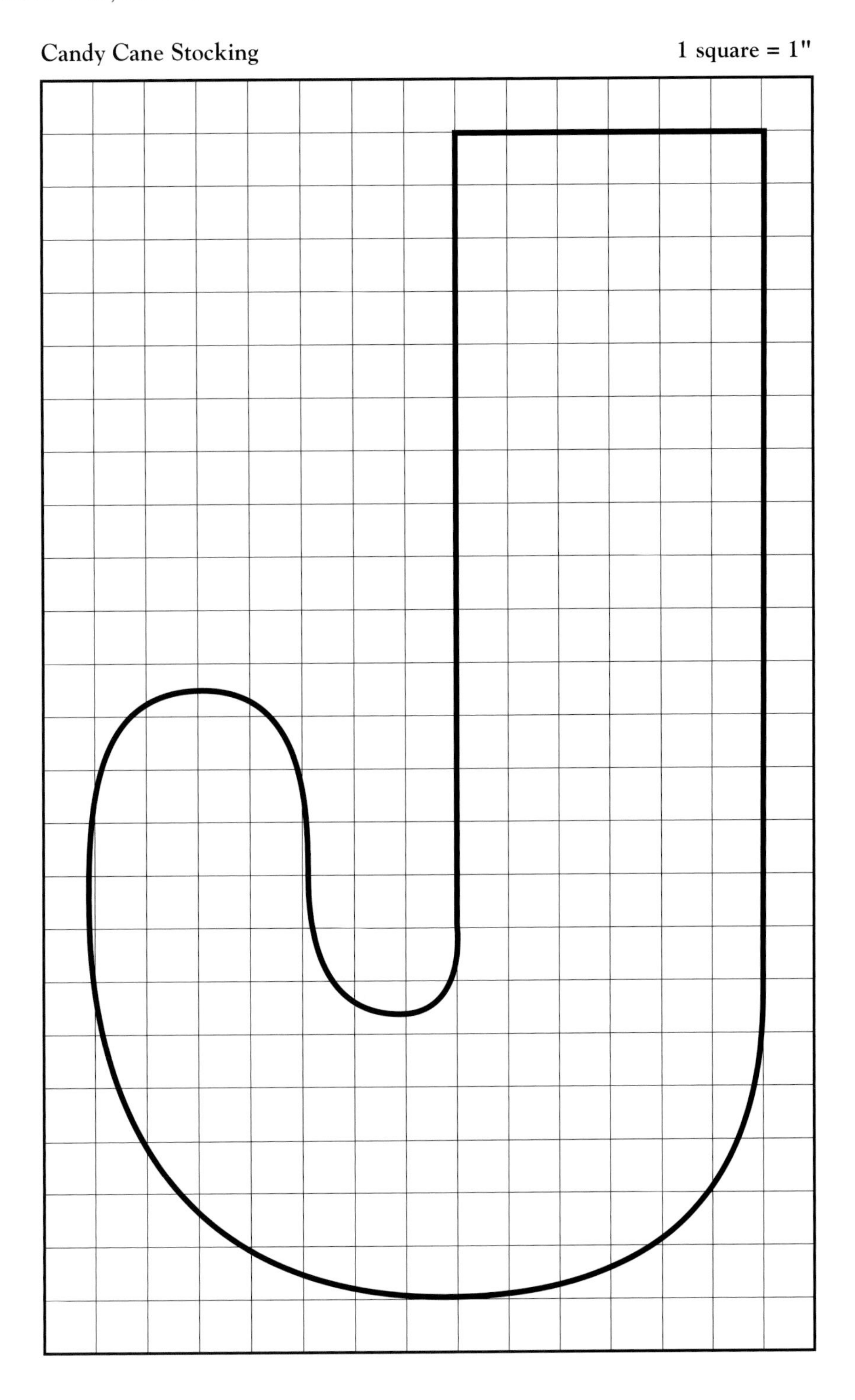

something for everyone (pages 52-61)

STARRY SCARF AND FANCIFUL HAT (continued)

Trimming: *Ball fringe "hat band"* – Pin around bottom edge of right side of hat, edges even; stitch. *Stars* – Pin to hat; hand-sew same as for scarf.

Stitching/attaching brim: Stitch short ends of each brim piece together, creating two circles. Pin circles together; stitch around outer edge. Clip curves; turn right side out; press. Stitch along open (inner) edge of brim to hold. Pin brim to hat, raw edges even; stitch close to fringe. Embroider edges with yellow blanket stitches.

Finishing: Roll down ears, back to back; hand-sew to secure.

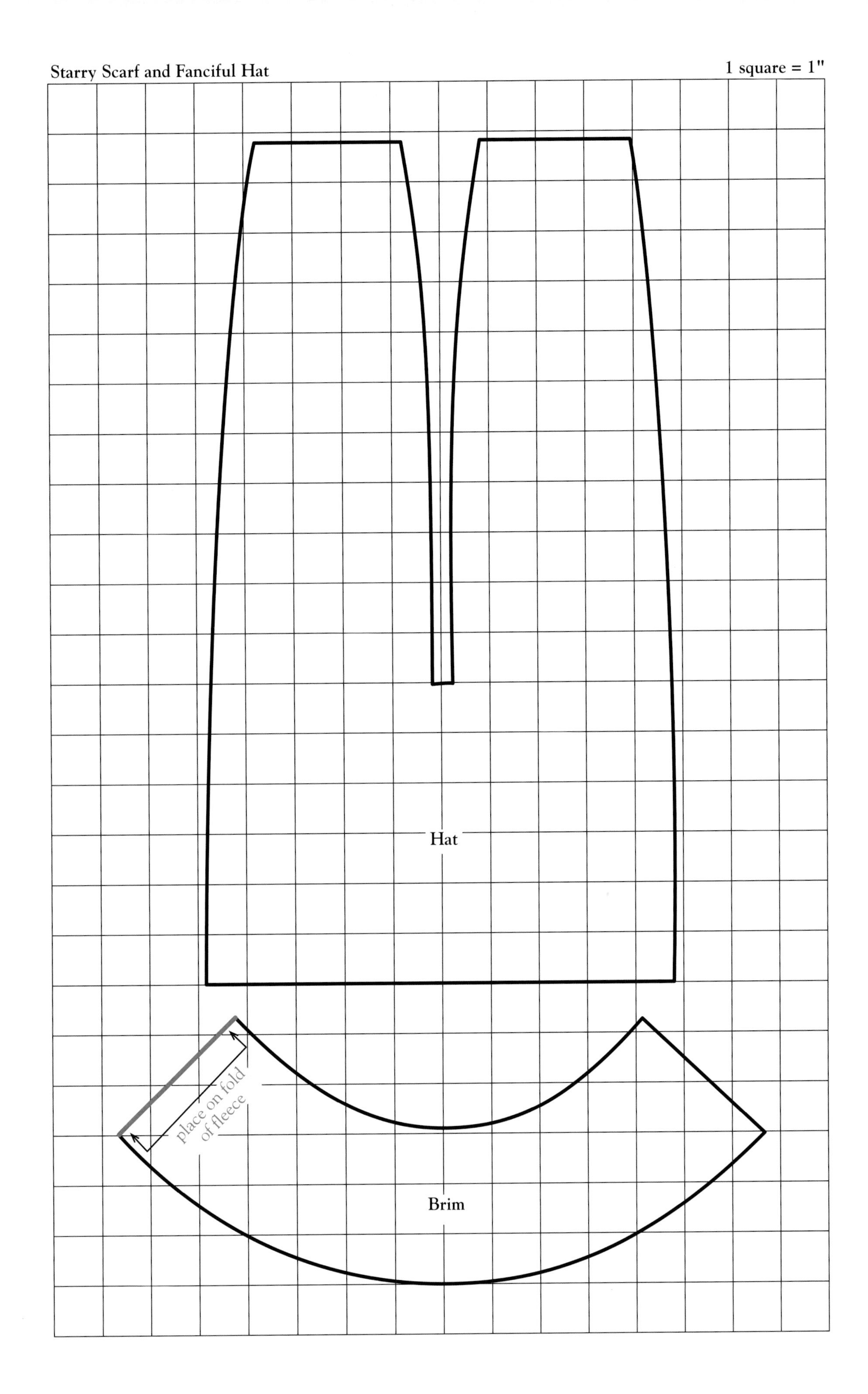
Starry Scarf and Fanciful Hat
1 square = 1"
Hat
place on fold
of fleece
Brim

KEEPSAKE NOTES

You need: Decorative papers; white paper (lining); assorted ribbons, beads, charms; glue stick; glue gun; embroidery floss. *Optional* – Purchased envelopes.
Making each card: From decorative paper, cut outer card to size desired (if sending, cut cards to fit purchased envelopes). Fold paper in half. Cut smaller appliqué pieces. From white paper, cut piece 1/4" smaller all around than outer card for lining; fold in half. Secure lining inside card with glue stick at folded edge.
Decorating: Using photo for inspiration, decorate card with papers, ribbons, and charms. Use glue stick to adhere papers and ribbon; use hot glue to adhere heavier items. On some cards, whipstitch edges of ribbon or paper with one strand of embroidery floss.

LADYBUG ORNAMENT

You need: 2" wooden half-egg; paintbrushes; acrylic paint – red, green, white; black structural paint; spring-type clothespin; glue gun.
Making ornament: Paint egg red; let dry. Paint black line down center of egg. Paint black dots on back and near one end for eyes; let dry. Paint white highlight on each eye. Paint clothespin green; let dry. Glue clothespin on back of ornament.

TINY TREE (continued)

Making second row: Cut five 12"L pieces of wire. On each, slip on 13 beads, center and twist ends together against beads for loop. Then slip 19 beads on end of one wire. Snug beads up against loop. Loop wire, wrapping end between the sixth and seventh beads away from first loop. Pull snug and twist, making second 13-bead loop. Repeat with other wire end. Next, slip six beads on each wire and twist ends together against beads. Twist entire piece around itself as before. Arrange branches evenly spaced around trunk 3/8" below previous row.
Making third row: Make same as second row, except slip seven beads on ends instead of six. Arrange around trunk 3/8" below previous row.
Making fourth row: Cut six 14"L pieces of wire. On each, slip on 13 beads, center and twist. On one end slip on 18 beads. Snug beads up against loop. Loop wire, wrapping end between the fifth and sixth beads away from first loop. Pull snug and twist, making second 13-bead loop. then slip on another 18 beads and repeat, making another loop on same wire. Repeat on other end of wire. There are five loops on this branch. Slip five beads on each wire and twist ends together. Twist piece around itself. Arrange branches around trunk 3/8" below previous row.
Making fifth row: Make same as fourth row except increase the 18 beads to 19, leaving six beads between the loops. Arrange branches around trunk 3/8" below previous row.
Making sixth row: Cut seven 14"L pieces of wire. On each, slip on 13 beads, center and twist. On one end slip on 20 beads. Snug beads up against loop. Loop wire, wrapping end between the seventh and eighth beads away from first loop. Pull snug and twist, making second 13-bead loop. Then slip on another 20 beads and repeat, making another loop on same wire. Repeat on other end of wire. There are five loops on this branch. Slip seven beads on each wire and twist ends together. Twist piece around itself. Arrange branches around trunk.
Making seventh row: Make same as sixth row, decreasing beads between loops from seven to six. Complete as before; arrange branches on trunk.
Finishing: Trim trunk to 2" below bottom row of branches; wrap with floral tape.
Painting flowerpot "stand": Paint pot gold; let dry. Cut a piece of floral form; insert in pot; secure with hot glue. Insert trunk; secure with hot glue.
Decorating: Using pliers, attach charms and ornaments to branches with jump rings. Glue rhinestone circle to large gold star charm with jewelry glue. Hot-glue star to tree top.

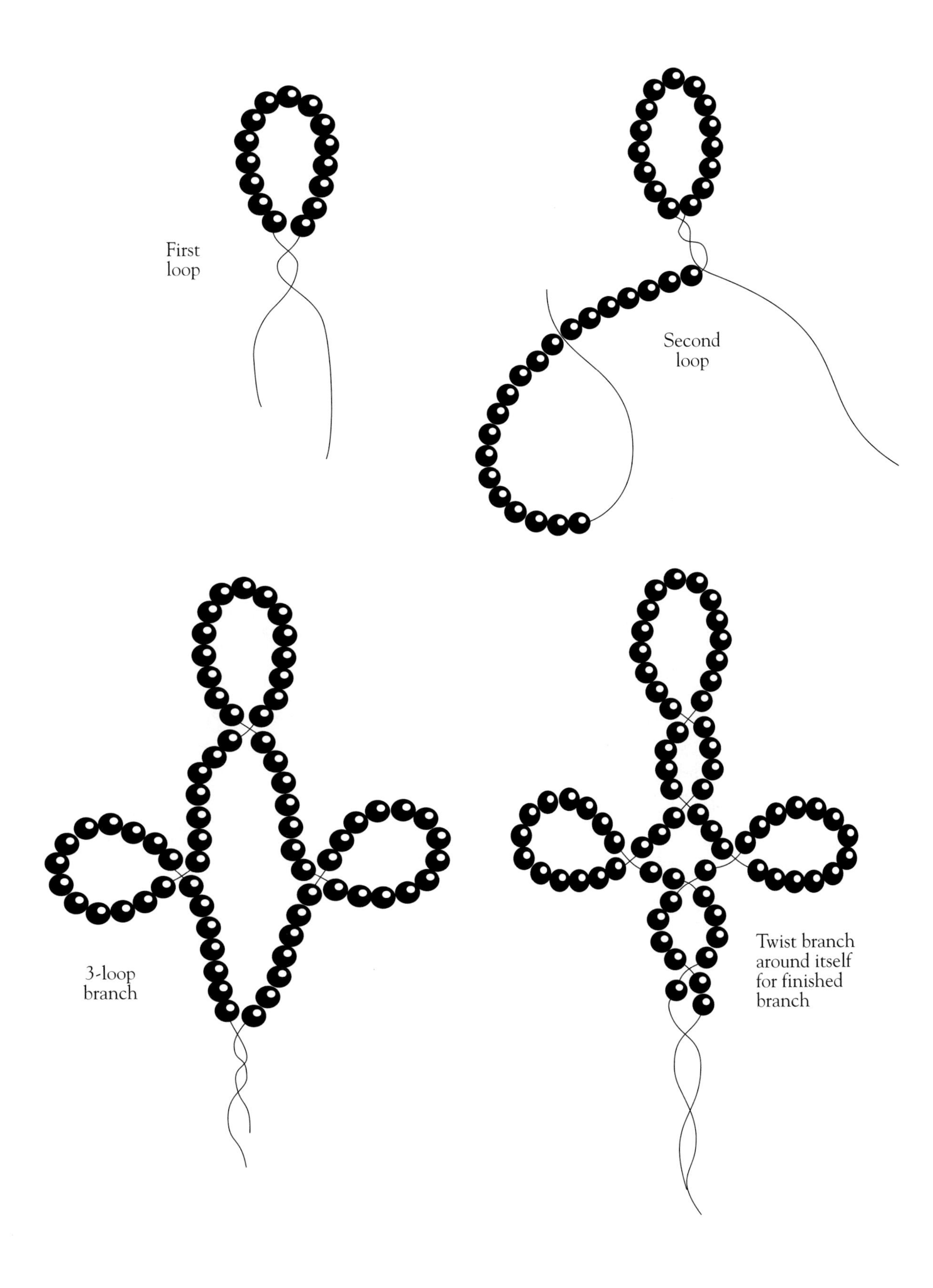
First
loop
Second
loop
3-loop
branch
Twist branch
around itself
for finished
branch

BERIBBONED PILLOWS

Size: 16" x 16" square and 7"H x 12"W

You need (for both): 1/2 yd of fusible web; ribbons (we used 1 1/2 yds each of 9 styles); 1/2 yd muslin; 1/2 yd velvet; fiberfill stuffing; 3 yds of trim; glue gun.

Either Pillow – Cutting fabric: With a 1/2" seam allowance all around, cut one piece each fusible web, muslin (top), and velvet (back) 17" x 17" square and 8"W x 13"L respectively.

Making pillow top: Place fusible web, paper side down, on table. Cut ribbons in pieces to equal the length of longest dimension (17"L and 13"L respectively). Arrange and pin ribbons on web (so web is completely covered); fuse. Peel off paper backing; fuse to muslin.

Finishing: Pin top and back together, right sides facing. Stitch 1/2" seam; leave opening for turning. Turn right side out; stuff firmly; slipstitch closed. Cut and hot-glue trim to fit around edges.

ROUND TREASURE BOX (continued)

Painting: Prime box/lid with gesso; let dry. *Lid/feet* – Paint light gold. With tip of brush handle, dot medium gold on lid and feet. Paint light purple stripes down lid lip; dry. Add a squiggly red line down each stripe. *Box* – Paint medium gold; dry. Brush lightly with light gold.

Decorating: Tear an oval from paper. Brush with decoupage medium; adhere (centered) on lid. Sponge on gold paint. Cut fabrics, ribbons; cut a small heart, then layer them attractively. Sew through all layers; sew on beads. Tie a gold-cord bow to loop on charm; glue to heart with fabric glue. Glue to lid with fabric glue.

HOLIDAY COCKTAIL GLASSES

You need: Clear glass cocktail glasses; paintbrushes – small shader, larger shader; gold glossy glass paint; translucent glass paint – red, yellow, green, blue.

Painting: Paint bands of color on outside of each glass, using small brush. Make each band same width as brush. Let each color dry before applying the next. Paint bases with large shader, using overlapping brush strokes.

Finishing: Follow paint manufacturer's instructions to heat-set paint.

"QUILTED" CAKE STAND

You need: Clear glass cake pedestal and dome; washable marker; straightedge; compass; paintbrushes – shader, round; translucent glass paints – red, yellow, green, blue.

Marking designs: Draw motifs on undersides of pedestal and dome with marker; use straightedge and compass as needed.

Painting: Dab on paint, using shader brush, following markings. Work from center outward. Use round brush to paint star motifs.

Finishing: Follow paint manufacturer's instructions to heat-set paint.

NIFTY MITTENS (continued)

Next rnd: Slip first 11 (13) sts to holder for thumb – 38 (44) sts. Work even for 2". ***Next rnd (dec rnd):*** [K1, sl 1, K1, psso, K13 (16), K2 tog, K1] twice. ***Next rnd:*** K all sts. Next rnd (dec rnd): [K1, sl 1, K1, psso, K11 (14), K2 tog, K1] twice. ***Next rnd:*** K all sts. Work dec rnd 2 (3) more times, working 2 fewer sts bet decs each rnd – 22 (24) sts. Bind off. Stitch opening with overcast sts.

Finishing thumb: Pick up 2 sts at top of thumb opening and thumb sts from holder – 13 (15) sts. Divide sts evenly on 3 needles. Work even for 1 1/2". ***Next rnd:*** [K1, K2 tog] 4 (5) times, K1 (0). Cut yarn; weave tail through sts.

Dotted Mitten

Work same shaping as Striped Mitten. Cast on and work ribbing and first 2 St st rows with G; change to R. Change to G for last 3 rnds of hand and last 2 rnds of thumb. Follow Dot Chart to stitch duplicate-st dots on back of hand.

Dotted Mitten – Dot Chart

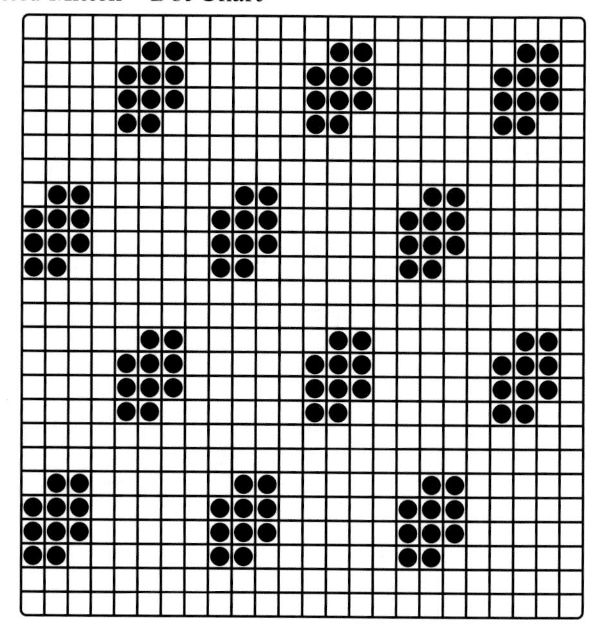

STUFFED SCOTTIE

You need: 1¼ yds red boiled wool or felt; 2 skeins black embroidery floss; 2 black buttons; fiberfill stuffing; 1 yd wide plaid ribbon.

Cutting: Enlarge pattern (below). Cut pattern twice from wool for front and back. Also cut 72" x 4" strip of wool for gusset.

Assembling: Sew on button eyes. Overlap short ends of gusset 1"; stitch ends together. Pin gusset to front, wrong sides facing; sew blanket stitches round edges to attach gusset to front. Pin other edge of gusset to back, wrong sides facing; stitch in same manner, leaving opening along bottom. Stuff; finish stitching around edge in same way.

Finishing: Tie ribbon bow around neck; trim ends.

TEDDY TOY

You need: ⅜ yd red boiled wool or felt; black embroidery floss; fiberfill stuffing.

Cutting: Enlarge pattern (page 154). From wool, cut two head sections (leave wool folded after cutting), two ears, two bodies, four arms, four legs, and two paws.

Stitching: *All pieces are blanket-stitched around edges with floss and stuffed before completing stitching.* Insert ears between head layers on sides of fold; stitch around head, starting and ending at fold edges. Stitch body sections and two pairs of arm sections together around edges to make body and two arms. Stitch two pairs of leg sections together along curved edges. Stitch paw to bottom of each leg.

Assembling: Sew head to top of body. Sew arms to body, just below head. Sew legs to sides of body.

Finishing: Embroider facial features.

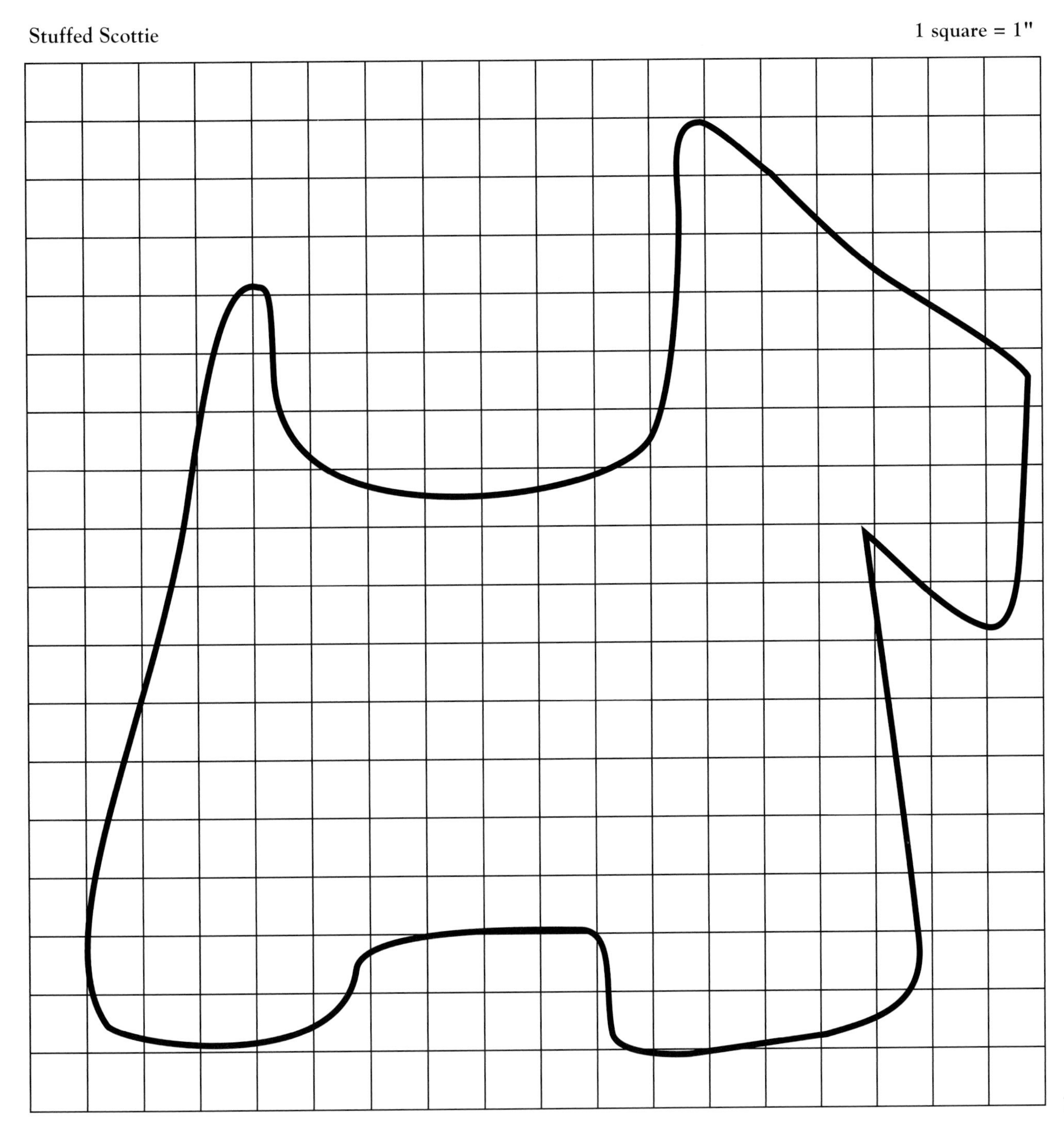

MERRY MARIONETTE

You need: 24" of 1/4" dowel; 12" of 3/4" dowel; two 1 5/8"L wooden eggs; craft sticks – 1 large, 2 small; drill with 1/4" and 1/16" bits; 6" x 14" piece of fabric; cotton string; paintbrush; permanent markers – black, red; green acrylic paint; pinking shears; green yarn; small bow; glue gun.

Preparing dowels: From 1/4" dowel, cut one 7 1/2" arm piece, two 6" legs, and one 3" hip. From 3/4" dowel, cut one 6 1/4" torso/head piece. Drill a 1/4" hole 2" from each end of torso and in each shoe as shown on page 60. Drill a 1/16" hole 1/2" from each end of arms, 1/4" from each end of hip, at one end and at center of each leg, at top of head, at each end of each small craft stick, and at center of large stick.

Assembling: Slip arms and hip through torso. Using short pieces of string, tie legs to ends of hip. Fold fabric in half crosswise, right side out; trim edges with pinking shears for costume. Cut slit in fold for neck; cut "U" shape at lower edge for legs. Slip costume onto body. Using string, stitch sides and inner legs. Paint shoes green; glue to ends of legs. Using markers, draw face. Form yarn into loops for hair, glue to top of head. Glue bow to neck.

Making marionette: Glue small craft sticks across ends of long craft stick to make handle. Cut five long pieces of string; tie one piece through each hole in doll. Slip strings through handle holes; tie each string to handle so doll hangs evenly and moves freely.

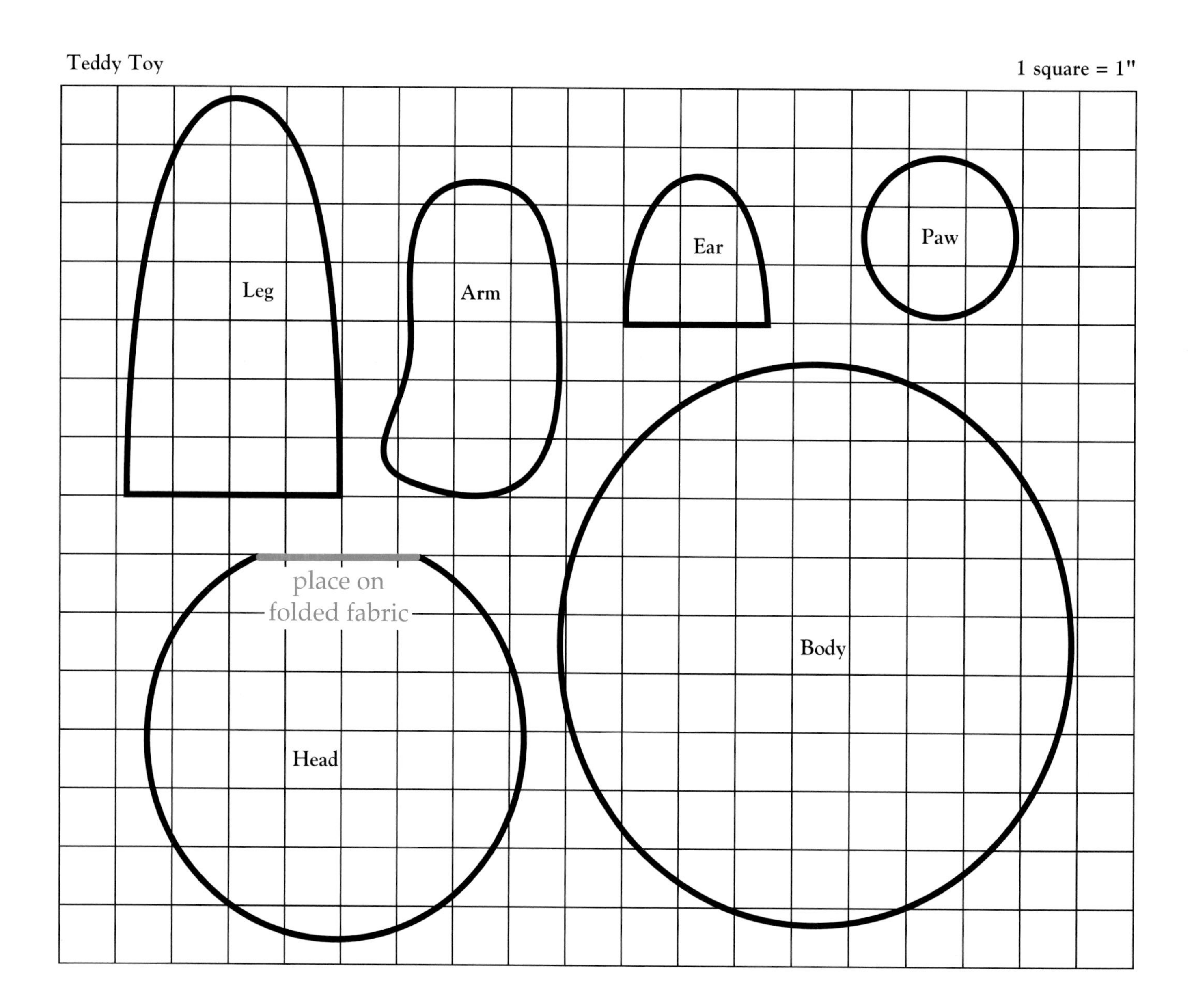

gifts of flavor

(page 66)

RIBBON BAGS

You need (for each): 1/2 yd of 5"W wired metallic ribbon; metallic thread; 3/4 yd of 1 1/4"W wired gold mesh ribbon; 1 1/8 yds gold braid; small glass ball ornament.

Making bag: Fold 5"W ribbon in half, wrong sides facing and matching ends. Use metallic thread to hand-stitch along wired edges.

Finishing: Place gift in bag. Cut braid in half; knot ends. Tie braid and mesh ribbon together in bow around bag, slipping ornament onto ribbon before completing bow.

home sweet homes

(pages 76-78)

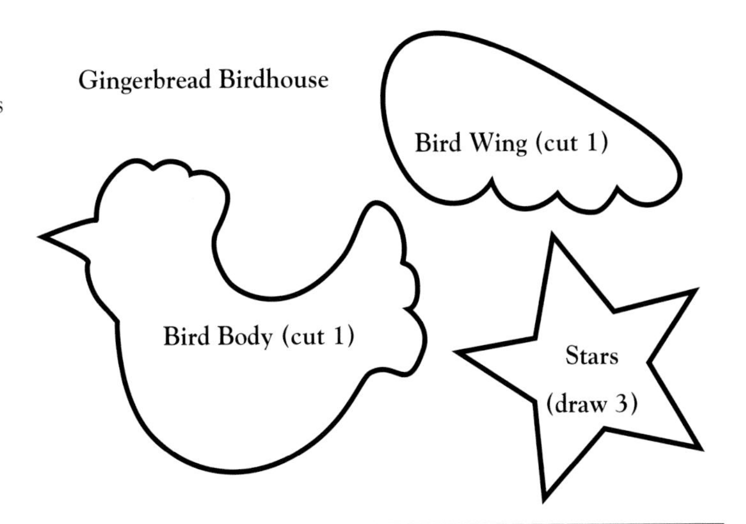

basic how-to's

How to Enlarge Patterns

We recommend making enlargements on a copier – it's fast and accurate. Use the "enlarge" button; repeat copying and enlarging until you get the desired size. For some patterns you may also use the grid method: Copy the pattern one square at a time onto 1" grid graph paper to get a full-size pattern.

Knit Abbreviations

bet – between
dec – decrease
dp – double–pointed
gr – grams
k – knit
mm – millimeters
p – purl
psso – pass slipped stitch over
rnd(s) – round(s)
sl – slip
St st – Stockinette stitch
st(s) – stitch(es)
tog – together

Embroidery

Blanket Stitch

A

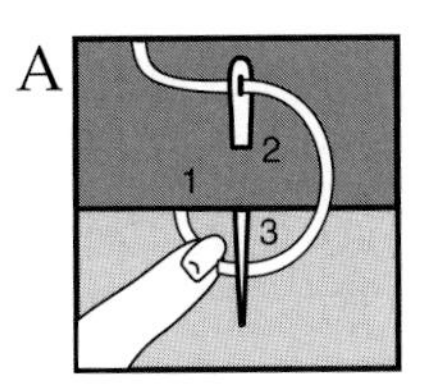

B

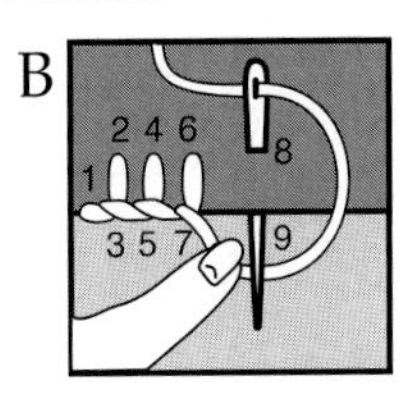

Cross Stitch

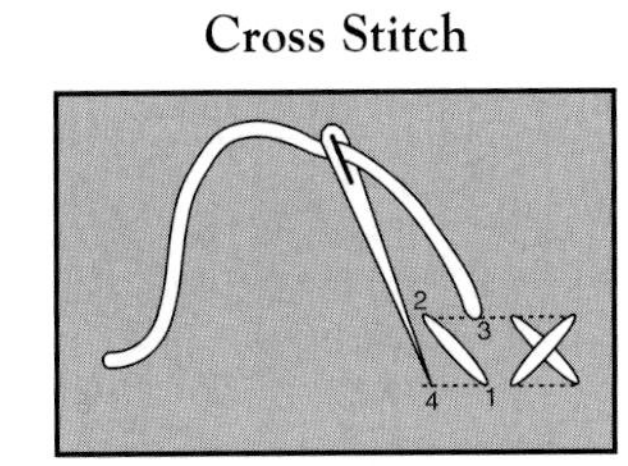

Satin Stitch

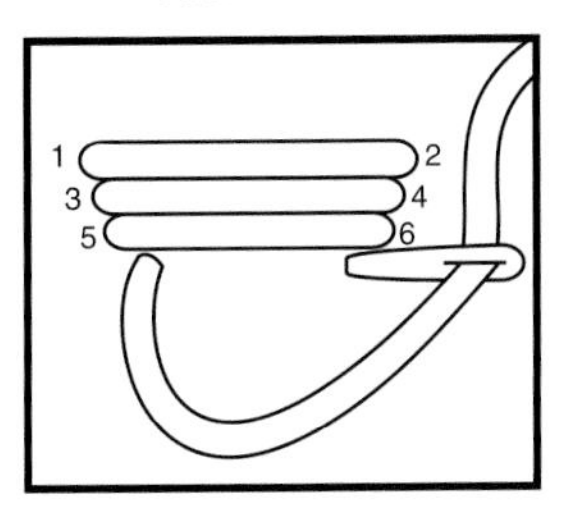

Chain Stitch

A

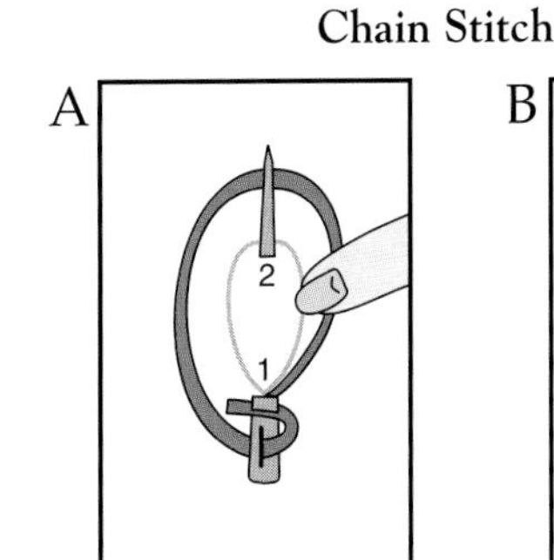

B

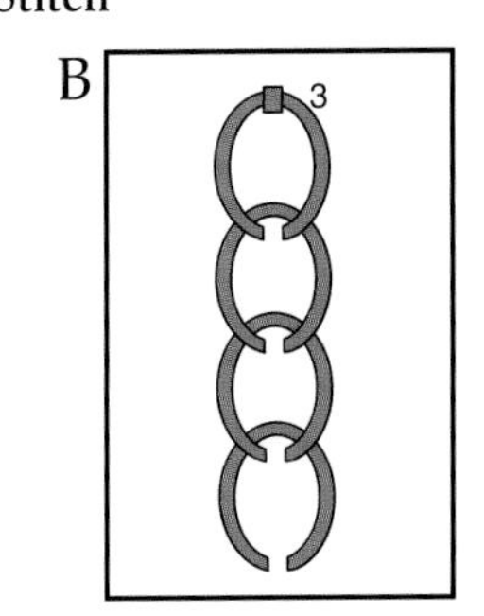

Duplicate Stitch

A

B

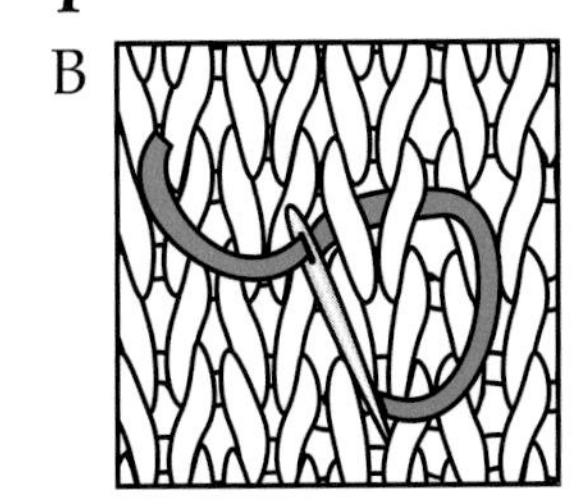

C

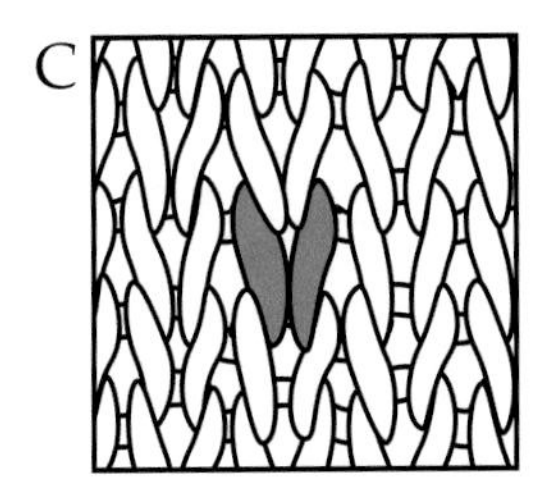

home sweet homes (pages 76-78)

Gingerbread Birdhouse (See How to Enlarge Patterns, page 155.) 1 square = 1"

how-to's index

Continued on page 158

recipe index

D-E

F

G

H-L

M

N-O

P-R

S

T-W

credits

To Magna IV Color Imaging of Little Rock, Arkansas, we say thank you for the superb color reproduction and excellent pre-press preparation.

To the talented people who helped create the following projects and recipes in this book, we extend a special word of thanks:

- Cheryl Ball: *Candy Ornaments*, pg. 47.
- Creative Windows: *Plaid Stocking, Pocket Stocking, Jester Stocking, Candy Cane Stocking*, pg. 45; *Beribboned Pillows*, pg. 55.
- Mary Ellen Cocci: *Starry Scarf and Fanciful Hat*, pg. 52.
- Denise Crolle-Terzaghi: *Keepsake Notes*, pg. 53.
- Jeanne Elliot: *Christmas Quilt*, pg. 21.
- Michele Filon: *Teddy Toy*, pg. 61.
- Stephanie Gildersleeve: *Nifty Mittens*, pg. 59.
- Gramercy Park Flower Shop: *All-Green Wreath*, pg. 11.
- Lori Hellander: *Frosty Snowmen*, pg. 17.
- Leslie Hemmings: *Bow-Trimmed Bootie, Linen Cuff Stocking, Patchwork Stocking, Pom-Pom Stocking*, pg. 17.
- Susan Hinckley: *Block Ornaments, Frosty Snowmen*, pg. 16; *Candy Cane Ornaments*, pg. 17; *Patchwork Album*, pg. 20; *Treasure Boxes*, pg. 56.
- Diane Hogle: *Advent Calendar*, pg. 12; *Velvet Pet Pillow, Treat Sack*, pg. 29.
- Margot Hotchkiss: *Ribbon Balls*, pg. 24; *Ribbon Rosettes*, pg. 26.
- Edward Kemper: *Fruit-and-Flower Pots*, pg. 34.
- Alice Koehler: *Christmas Throw*, pg. 28.
- Kim Kushner: *Star Tree Topper, Cinnamon Stick Bundles, Fruit Pomanders*, pg. 47; *Button-Rich Wreath*, pg. 54.
- Amy Leonard: *Holiday Napkins*, pg. 18.
- Amy Marciano: *Crocheted Bonnets*, pg. 26.
- Lina Morielli: *Butler Claus*, pg. 44.
- Helen Raffles: *Cookie Cottage Ornaments*, pg. 49.
- Sheila Haynes Rauen: *Star-Stamped Gift Paper*, pg. 39; *Painted Christmas Balls*, pg. 41; *Holiday Cocktail Glasses, Quilted Cake Stand*, pg. 57.
- Carole Rodgers: *Tiny Tree*, pg. 54.
- Roy Rudin: *Hankie Pillows*, pg. 16; *Victorian Tree Skirt*, pg. 27.
- Deborah Schneebeli-Morrell: *Silver Crackers*, pg. 43.
- Daphne Shirley & Sarah Shirley: *Brocade Boot, High-Button Shoe, Fringe Bootie, Silk and Pearl Stocking*, pg. 23.
- Susan Miller Smith: *North Star*, pg. 6; *Fabulous Floral Wreath*, pg. 11.
- Arlene Hamilton Stewart: *Silvery Bead Ornaments*, pgs. 38 and 41.
- Allison Stilwell: *Ladybug Ornament*, pg. 53.
- Andrea Swenson: *Teddy Ornaments*, pg. 46.
- Karen Tack: *Frosted Gingerbread Castle*, pg. 42.
- Robin Tarnoff: *Snow Dolls*, pg. 13; *Pony Ornaments*, pg. 15; *Celestial Ornaments*, pg. 41; *Stuffed Scottie*, pg. 61.
- Cindy Tower: *Lace Garland*, pg. 47.
- Douglas Turshen & Rochelle Udell: *Bauble Star Door Decoration*, pg. 40.
- Jim Williams: *Fabric Globes*, pg. 15; *Santa and Santa's Helper Aprons*, pg. 19; *Crocheted Angels, Brocade Doves*, pg. 26; *Host and Hostess Vests*, pg. 58.
- Excerpted from **The Family Circle Cookbook: New Tastes for New Times**, by the Editors of Family Circle and David Ricketts © 1992 by The Family Circle, Inc.: *Roasted Red-Pepper Dip, Salsa Fresca*, and *Spinach-Feta-Cheese Dip*, pg. 72; *Maple Cider Toddy*, pg. 83; *Frothy Mexi-Mocha Coffee*, pg. 86.
- And of course, special thanks to the expertise of the *Family Circle* Food Department.

Special acknowledgment is given to the following *Family Circle* photographers:

- Antonis Achilleos: pgs. 13, 57, 62, 63; bottom, pg. 64; left, pg. 66; pg. 67; top, pg. 70; pgs. 71, 109.
- John Bessler: pgs. 12, 14-17; bottom, pg. 53; pg. 58.
- Monica Buck: pg. 6; top, pg. 11; pg. 19; top, pg. 29; pg. 31.
- Monica Buck from *Gifts of Nature*. Available from Clarkson N. Potter Publishers, NY: pg. 30.
- Steve Cohen: pg. 18; bottom, pg. 75.
- Lydia Gould: pg. 45; pg. 46; pgs. 47, 50-51.
- Brian Hagiwara: top, pg. 64; pgs. 65, 69; bottom, pg. 70; pgs. 88, 91, 94, 95, 113, 115-117.
- Bill Holt: pg. 44.
- Paul Kopelow: pgs. 40-41.
- Kevin Lein: pg. 10.
- Michael Luppino: bottom, pg. 11; pg. 32; top, pg. 33; pgs. 42-43.
- Peter Margonelli: pgs. 38-39.
- Steven Mays: pg. 8; pgs. 22-28; bottom, pg. 29.
- Jeff McNamara: top, pg. 20; pg. 21.
- Steven Mark Needham: pgs. 72, 92.
- Randy O'Rourke: pg. 76.
- Steve Randazzo: top, pg. 53; pgs. 54-56, 61.
- Alan Richardson: pgs. 34, 49, 73; top, pg. 75; pgs. 80, 82; left, pg. 83; pgs. 84, 87, 96, 98, 100-108, 110-112, 114.
- Monica Stevenson: pg. 79.
- Ross Whitaker: pg. 52.
- Reprinted from *Gifts From Nature: Topiaries and Pomanders*. Available from Lorenz Books, NY: left, pg. 37.
- Reprinted from *Spicecrafts*. Available from Lorenz Books, NY: pg. 36.

We also wish to thank the following *Family Circle* photography stylists:

- Betty Alfenito: pgs. 63, 100-107, 109, 111.
- Denise Carter: pgs. 108, 110.
- Cathy Cook: pgs. 84, 91; bottom, pg. 94; pgs. 112, 114.
- Julie Gong: bottom, pg. 75.
- Edward Kemper Design: pg. 62; bottom, pg. 64; pg. 67; top, pg. 70; pgs. 71, 73; top, pg. 75; pgs. 80, 82; left, pg. 83; pgs. 87, 96, 98.
- Francine Matalon-Degni: pg. 92.
- Christine McCabe: top, pg. 64; pgs. 65, 88; top, pg. 94; pgs. 95, 113, 115-117.
- Faith Meade: top, pg. 64; pg. 69; bottom, pg. 70.
- Lisa Sacco: pgs. 76, 79.

Thanks also go to the following *Family Circle* food stylists:

- A. J. Battifarano: pgs. 64, 65, 69, 70, 84, 88, 113, 115-117.
- Roscoe Betsill: pg. 112.
- Cathy Cook: pgs. 63, 109.
- Anne Disrude: pgs. 100-107.
- Susan Ehlich: bottom, pg. 75.
- Elaine Khosrova: top, pg. 94; pg. 95.
- Karen Tack: pg. 62; bottom, pg. 64; pg. 67; top, pg. 70; pgs. 71, 111.
- Fred Thompson: pg. 91; bottom, pg. 94.
- William Smith: pg. 73; top, pg. 75; pgs. 80, 82; left, pg. 83; pgs. 87, 96, 98, 108, 110, 114.
- Andrea Swenson: pg. 92.